Gessar Khan
A LEGEND OF TIBET

Gessar Khan
A LEGEND OF TIBET

Told by
IDA ZEITLIN

Illustrated by
THEODORE NADEJEN

PILGRIMS PUBLISHING
◆Varanasi◆

GESSAR KHAN
A Legend of Tibet
IDA ZEITLIN

Published by:
PILGRIMS PUBLISHING

An imprint of:
PILGRIMS BOOK HOUSE
(Distributors in India)
B 27/98 A-8, Nawabganj Road
Durga Kund, Varanasi-221010, India
Tel: 91-542-2314059, 2314060, 2312456
Fax: 91-542-2312788, 2311612
E-mail: pilgrims@satyam.net.in
Website: www.pilgrimsbooks.com

PILGRIMS BOOK HOUSE (New Delhi)
9 Netaji Subhash Marg, 2nd Floor
Near Neeru Hotel, Daryaganj, New Delhi 110002
Tel: 91-11-23285081
E-mail: pilgrim@del2.vsnl.net.in

Distributed in Nepal by:
PILGRIMS BOOK HOUSE
P O Box 3872, Thamel, Kathmandu, Nepal
Tel: 977-1-4700942, Off: 977-1-4700919, Fax: 977-1-4700943
E-mail: pilgrims@wlink.com.np

First Published in 1927
Copyright © 2004, Pilgrims Publishing
All Rights Reserved

Cover design by Sasya
Illustrated by Theodore Nadejen

ISBN: 81-7769-084-1

Printed in India at Pilgrim Press Pvt. Ltd. Lalpur Varanasi

PREFACE TO THE NEW EDITION

Gessar-Khan was the mythical hero of Tibet and also well loved amongst the nomadic Mongolian tribes who roamed the steppes of central Asia. Tales of his exploits were carried by word of mouth and related orally for centuries by these people around their campfires and during the long and cold winter nights. These legendary tales first appeared in the Mongolian language at the order of the Chinese Emperor Kanghi in about 1716.

Much later in 1836 Issac Jakob Schmidt was authorized to translate them and present them to the Imperial Academy Of Sciences in St. Petersburg. Even later in 1839 Professor Schmidt translated them into his native German presenting them under the title of *Die Thaten Bogda Gesser Chans*. It is from this version that Ida Zeitlin translated the English edition. It was only after the publication of the German edition that a great interest began to develop in the Western world thus making the English edition a must.

Tales of monsters, demons dragons and maidens in distress, which have always filled people with delight, fill these pages to entertain and enlighten the reader. Whether these tales originated in Tibet or in Mongolia has never been ascertained but whatever the origins they do not fail to entertain readers of all ages, irrespective of where they may come from. This well illustrated book provides us with a great deal of insight into the hopes and fears of a people who have always remained an enigma to the world.

Christopher N Burchett
June 2003
Varanasi

FOREWORD

In Peking in 1716, during the reign of Kanghi and at his order, there appeared in the Mongolian language the legend of Gessar Khan, mythical hero of Asia, whose mighty exploits had lived long on the lips of the people before they were set forth in print. in 1836 the Imperial Academy of Sciences in St. Petersburg authorized Isaac Jakob Schmidt, one of its members, to prepare a new edition in Mongolian from the earlier text, and three years later sanctioned a project apparently very close to Professor Schmidt's heart, a German translation. It is upon this German translation, entitled *Die Thaten Bogda Gesser Chans* and published in St. Petersburg in 1839, that the present version is principally based, although reference has also been made to Benjamin Bergmann's account of the so-called Little Gesser, translated from a Kalmuck original, and included in *Nomadische Streifereien*, Volume III, published in Riga in 1804.

Whether the origin of the epic is Tibetan or Mongolian is not clear, since it has been set down in both languages, but Professor Schmidt inclined to the former view through the weight of internal evidence. Himself a student and lover of Oriental lore, he saw in this work a source of living material, hitherto inaccessible to Europeans, on the modes of speech and manners of life of the nomad indifferent to the treasure of pure folk narrative he had made available, and of which this volume seeks to take advantage.

IDA ZEITLIN.
244 Madison Avenue,
New York City
September, 1927

CONTENTS

I. THE HERO'S BIRTH

OF THE HERO'S BIRTH AND THE STRANGE EVENTS THAT PRECEDED IT, AND OF THOSE WONDROUS EXPLOITS OF HIS YOUTH WHEREIN HIS MAGIC POWERS WERE REVEALED.

Kormuzda, father of the gods, ruler over the high heavens and guardian of the earth, went down from his place on Sumeru, and knelt in worship at the feet of Buddha, fountain of good and light of all the world.

And when he had bowed his head nine times upon the lowest step of Buddha's throne, the master spoke: "Thy homage, noblest of the gods, is sweet as the breatn of incense in my nostrils. Hear now my word. Return to Sumeru, and for five hundred years let joy and feasting rule in thy domain. But when those years are spent, forsake thy revelry, for an evil day shall dawn on the sons of men. Brother shall arm himself against his brother, the beasts of the wilderness devour their mates, pastures and rivers shall be stained with blood, and like a rootless tree sweet peace shall perish. When that day dawns, let one of thy three sons descend in mortal guise to rule the earth, that the tenfold evil may be destroyed and gladness restored to the hearts of men."

And the god Kormuzda bowed his head upon the lowest step of Buddha's throne, and returned to his dwelling-place. And for five hundred years he feasted among the three and thirty gods that served his will, but when those years were spent, he had forgot the command of the Lord Buddha, and feasted for another hundred years and for another.

And suddenly a roar shattered the heavens, as though ten thousand dragons called to one another, and all amazed, Kormuzda saw how the great wall that guarded his kingdom on the west shuddered and fell and crumbled into ruin.

And he was wroth, and laying hold upon his weapon, he cried: "What foe ventures to storm the walls of the high gods? Let him appear, and though he be the fifteen-headed dragon, or lord of the Assuri of evil fame, I will challenge him to combat, and he that is the victor, let him rule henceforth in triumph over my domain."

But none gave answer to his challenge, and advancing

upon the shattered wall that even now had towered in majesty, he saw that no enemy had stormed it, neither the fifteen-headed dragon, nor the Assuri that dwell about the foot of Sumeru and strive in ancient enmity against the gods.

And suddenly in anguish Kormuzda cried: "It is thy hand, thou All-Seeing One, that hath chastened me! For didst thou not command me, after the passage of five hundred years, to send one of my sons to earth, that the tenfold evil might be destroyed and gladness restored to the hearts of men? And now seven hundred years have run their course and still they abide in ease on Sumeru!"

And he sent a messenger to seek his sons, and first the messenger came to Ameen, Kormuzda's eldest-born, and spoke to him, saying: "Belovèd of thy sire! Kormuzda bids thee descend to earth to rule in wisdom over the tribes of men!"

And Ameen made reply: "I am unschooled in wisdom, unfit to rule over the tribes of men. And how would the dear name and fair repute of heaven's lord be shamed, were I, his son, to essay this task and fail! Nay, for the great love that I bear my father, I may not do his bidding!"

And the messenger took his way to Weele, Kormuzda's second son, and spoke to him, saying: "Belovèd of thy sire! Kormuzda bids thee descend to earth to rule in wisdom over the tribes of men!"

And Weele answered: "I am the son of a mighty god, and these creatures that crawl upon the surface of the earth are men. What is their doom to me? Let Ameen descend

13

to do our father's bidding, for it is meet that the eldest-born should be first in deeds of valor. Or if it be his pleasure, let Tagus descend. I yield my right to him. But as for me, I have no liking for this enterprise, and I will not go!"

And now the messenger betook himself to Tagus, Kormuzda's youngest son, and spoke to him, saying: "Belovèd of thy sire! Kormuzda bids thee descend to earth to rule in wisdom over the tribes of men!"

And Tagus answered: "Why dost thou come to me with Kormuzda's word? Shall I usurp the duty of my brothers? My heart is clamorous and my feet impatient to do my father's bidding, yet I fear to bring dishonor on the heads of those to whom my love is due."

And the messenger returned and made known to Kormuzda the words that his sons had spoken. And Kormuzda, seated in splendor amid the three and thirty gods that served his will, bade his sons appear before him. And he said to them: "When I commanded you, belovèd sons, to sojourn upon the earth, that ye might cleanse it of corruption and rule in wisdom over the tribes of men, this was done not to please my fancy, but in obedience to the will of the Shining One. I counted you hitherto my children, but now it doth appear ye are my sire, and I your duteous son. Take therefore my place on Sumeru, attire yourselves in my royal robes and my crown, assume Kormuzda's majesty and might, and lay your commands upon him!"

And his three sons bowed their bright heads before Kormuzda's wrath, crying: "Wherefore does the prince of heaven pierce our hearts with words of bitterness?"

14

And Ameen the first-born said: "Well do I know that this task is greater than my strength, and therefore I denied thee, sire. For men would cry: 'This braggart boasts himself Kormuzda's son, and comes to be our lord! Yet his sword is powerless, and his puny arm falters before the onslaughts of our enemy. Kormuzda's son, forsooth! Ho, what a god is this that breeds such weaklings!'"

Then Weele spoke, saying: "When the seventeen gods of great Iswara's realm meet on the field, that they may vie with one another in feats of skill and valor, whose arrow speeds so swiftly to the mark as the arrow of Tagus? When the dragon-princes of the deep contend together for the crown of might, which of them all can measure his strength against the strength of Tagus? And when the three and thirty chosen ones that surround thy throne, thou ruler in the heavens, summon their brethren to a trial of arms, what blade is there that can prevail over the wonder-working blade of Tagus, our brother and thy youngest son? Then let Tagus descend to do the will of Buddha, for he alone of thy sons is worthy to bear thy mantle in the sight of men!"

And those that stood about Kormuzda's throne cried: "This is the very truth!"

And now Kormuzda bent his gaze upon his youngest son and cried: "Wilt thou undertake this task, thou whom thy comrades have named most valiant among them?"

And Tagus answered: "I will undertake it."

"What treasures wilt thou choose of my goodly store that thy labors upon earth may be lightened?"

"Thine armor that is fashioned of seven jewels and sparkles like the dew at dawn; thy helmet that is wrought of the woven light of the sun and moon; thy lightning-sword three fathoms long and thine ebon bow, with thirty silver arrows notched in turquoise."

"They shall be thine!"

"Let three of the dakeeni be born of the mother that shall bear me, and let them mount again to Sumeru and look down upon me, to turn my footsteps from peril."

"This shall be done, and Amurtsheela, daughter of Bayan, shall give you birth."

"Let one of the best-loved of all thy kin dwell at my side, that he may be my chosen friend and my heart's brother."

"This shall be done, and Sanglun, prince of Tussa, shall father him."

"Let thirty of the lesser gods follow me to earth, to be my comrades and a staff in my right hand, and from the heavenly herds bestow upon me thy brown wonder-steed, for he is a steed of might that will outstrip the torrent and overtake the fox and antelope. These treasures do I choose of thy goodly store, that my labors upon earth may be lightened."

"These treasures shalt thou have! Go now to prepare thyself for mortal birth, Tagus, Kormuzda's child, that shall be known to men as Yoro till thy fifteenth year be passed, and then as Gessar Khan, the son of heaven, lord of the ten great regions of the earth, bane of all evil and minister of Buddha to mankind."

And Tagus bade the assembled gods farewell, then

bowed before his father, and went to prepare himself for mortal birth.

Now in Tibet there dwelt two mighty princes, and one was Sanglun the Good that ruled over Tussa's tribe, and one was his brother Chotong of the false heart, that ruled over the tribe of Lik.

And Chotong came one day before his brother and said: "Let us make war upon Bayan our neighbor and seize his lands, for he plots evil against us. And when we have overthrown him, I will share with thee his people and his herds. But his daughter, Amurtsheela the Fair, shall be my prize."

And they rode against Bayan. And Sanglun rode to the fore and Chotong behind him, but when the encampment was destroyed and the warriors slain and the people put to rout, Chotong galloped to the head of the forces with a loud cry. And Amurtsheela fled before him, but stumbling in her flight, she dealt herself a grievous wound and was taken captive.

Then Chotong, black of heart, betrayed his brother, and took unto himself the flocks and lands and all the spoils of battle. And he cried to Sanglun: "I will give thee Amurtsheela, brother, to comfort thee. For she is lame of her wound, and, like an agèd crone she drags her limbs, and I will have none of her."

And Sanglun took pity upon Amurtsheela and gave her shelter within his yurta, and when her hurt was healed, she walked lightly as a soft-footed doe, fairest among the daughters of Tibet.

And now Chotong cast envious eyes upon her, and

would have taken her into his household, but she denied him. And hatred filled his breast, and going secretly among his people, he whispered to them: "The evil that is fallen on mankind springs from the union of Sanglun with Amurtsheela."

And the people cried: "Let them perish for the evil that is come upon us!"

And Chotong summoned them before him, and his voice flowed like honey from the comb. And he said: "The tribesmen clamor for thy death, Sanglun, and for thine, Amurtsheela. Yet I, being merciful, will spare your lives and sentence you instead to banishment where the three rivers meet. There ye may gather firewood to warm you, and out of my goodness I will bestow upon you a piebald camel and her colt, a dappled mare and her foal, a mottled cow and her heifer, a spotted ewe and her lambkin. And thy wealth shall be mine, Sanglun, and Rongsa and Shikeer, thy sons, shall serve me as my vassals."

And Sanglun went with Amurtsheela to the place where three rivers meet, and Amurtsheela gathered firewood to warm them, and Sanglun led their beasts to pasture, and hunted mountain hares that they might eat.

And on an evening when the moon was new, and Amurtsheela took her way home from the forest, a voice spoke in her ear: "Thou god-appointed one! At the full moon thou shalt bear three daughters, and a son destined for lofty deeds!" And the voice ceased from speaking, and Amurtsheela went on her way.

And when the moon was full, she said to Sanglun: "Go

19

not abroad on the morrow, I pray thee, Sanglun, for my heart is filled with strange forebodings, and I would have thee by me to cheer my solitude."

But he answered: "Nay, if I sit idle by thy side, how shall our food be snared, and our few sorry beasts be pastured? Take heart, fair Amurtsheela, for naught can harm thee."

And the day broke and waxed and waned, and at nightfall Amurtsheela the Fair bore three daughters, and their beauty was as the brightness of clear crystal, and as the burning of a radiant flame.

And now the sound of crashing cymbals filled the air and the beat of drums, and three elephants, saddled in gold and bridled in the blue that lights the heavens, descended on clouds of incense. And they knelt before the daughters of Amurtsheela who, mounted on their backs, soared upward to Sumeru.

And Amurtsheela wept bitterly, crying: "Woe, woe is me! Wherefore have ye taken my daughters from me, ye shining gods, ere yet I had clasped them to my breast or kissed their brows?"

And as she mourned thus, a voice within her cried: "Let me come forth, good mother!"

And from beneath her arm a son was born, and his right eye looked askance, but his left eye gazed truly before him. And he brandished his right hand fiercely above his head, but his left hand was balled into a fist, and his right foot was turned up, and his left foot down, and five and forty teeth were clenched in his mouth.

And Amurtsheela lifted up her voice and cried: "What monster is this that issues from my body, and gazes at me with a glance awry?"

And standing before her, he cried in a tiger's voice: "My eye that looks askance uncovers all the mischief that is wrought by mighty shimnus. My forward-gazing eye pierces the mystery of what has been and what is yet to be. My right hand, raised aloft, bids my foe beware, while my left hand, clenched together, bears witness that no enemy of the gods shall escape my wrath. One foot points downward in token that unrighteousness shall be crushed beneath its heel, and one points up to proclaim to all mankind that Buddha's law shall be exalted to the skies. And for my five and forty gnashing teeth, these are a sign that in the end all evil shall be swallowed up in me."

But Amurtsheela cried: "Alas, in Tibet a seemly babe is born with ears that hear not and a silent tongue. Yet thou dost wrangle with me, thou child of sorrow, ere thou hast dwelt an hour upon earth."

And now Sanglun, driving his meagre herd before him and bearing on his back the mountain hares he had taken in his net, approached the yurta and heard from within the clamor now of a woman's voice, now of a tiger's. And entering in, he cried: "What clamor is this that rings to the shores of the sea?"

And Amurtsheela answered: "Did I not bid thee stay by me, Sanglun, to shelter me from harm? See now what is befallen. I bore three daughters, children of the gods, yet hardly were they issued from my body, when three elephants descended out of the skies with incense and the beating of many drums and tore them from my arms. Straightway thereafter appeared this demon's spawn that brawls and glowers and brandishes his arms and makes as though he would devour me with his five and forty teeth."

"Nay, how canst thou know that a demon sired him and not a god? For look on this treasure I have taken of fourscore mountain hares, all in the single hour since his birth, though never before have I brought thee more than seven. It may be that I laid the snares more cunningly than I am wont, or it may be that the child is blessed of heaven. Wherefore let us feed and shelter him and name him with the name of Yoro."

And they named him with the name of Yoro, and he throve and kept the herds of Sanglun—the piebald camel and her colt, the dappled mare and her foal, the mottled cow and her heifer, the speckled ewe and her lambkin. And as they grazed one day, he plucked three golden reeds out of the earth, and three tall nettles, and three blades of grass, and three stalks of the karagana weed.

And with the karagana weed he struck the camel and cried: "Be fruitful, camel, and bear young plentifully as the steppes bear weeds!"

And he struck the mare with the blades of grass and cried: "Bring forth a horde of foals that shall outnumber the grasses of the plains!"

And the cow he struck with the tall nettles and cried: "Let thy seed be as the thorns on nettle-stalks!"

And with the golden reeds he struck the ewe, crying:

"A golden lamb be thine for every reed that ripens in the sun!"

And they did his bidding. And Amurtsheela rejoiced in the power of her son, and Sanglun rejoiced in the richness of his flocks.

And he cried: "I have heard it told that a thousand shall be born of one, but never till now have I beheld it. Yet who will tend these flocks, my Yoro, that are grown too numerous for thy keeping?"

And Yoro cried: "Behold, Sanglun!" And Sanglun saw that two riders galloped swiftly over the plain, and when they drew nigh, he knew them for his sons, Shikeer and Rongsa. And they knelt at his feet and cried: "We are escaped from the bondage of Chotong and come to seek thee."

And Sanglun raised them from the ground and bade them welcome.

And now the three youths tended the herds and drove them forth to pasture and dwelt in friendship together, until one day his brothers beheld how Yoro fell upon nine wethers and slaughtered them, and drew the skin from their bodies and cast the flesh into an earthen vessel. But the bones he gathered together, and laid each wether's bones within his skin.

And he built a fire beneath the vessel and, scattering incense, cried: "Kormuzda, noble god and well-loved father, and ye chosen ones that stand about his throne! Ye dragon princes of the deep! Ye deities of the realm of great Iswara! Give ear to me, for I am Tagus, born among men

23

according to the word of the Lord Buddha and at your bidding. In this poor body is my spirit housed, and with this sacrifice do I proclaim myself your servant and your son!"

And the gods cried to one another: "It is Tagus that calls upon us! Let him not call in vain!" And they put off the shining shapes of their godhood, and habited as mortals, they left their abode to partake of Yoro's sacrifice. And Yoro welcomed them and led them to the feast, and Shikeer gazed upon them, saying naught. But Rongsa fled away like a gazelle that is pursued by hounds.

And bursting in upon his father, he cried: "Yoro hath slain nine wethers of the flock and cast the flesh into an earthen vessel, and rends the air with strange and foolish sounds, as yea and yea, and gods from above and buddhas from below and dragons of the deep and boo and boo, and more of this that I cannot recall. And presently in answer to his cries came a throng of horsemen, whom he welcomed with loud acclaim and led to the feast, and now I make no doubt they have devoured the last sweet morsel of thy goodly rams."

And the wrath of Sanglun knew no bounds, and seizing his lash, he cried: "Yoro shall answer to me for this offense."

But when his guests had eaten their fill and returned to the skies, Yoro had swung the skin of each slaughtered ram thrice round his head, and lo! they stood quietly among their fellows and cropped the pasture. And he drove them homeward, and his brother Shikeer walked by his side.

And Sanglun came to meet them, but when he would

have fallen upon them Yoro wrested the lash from his grasp, and flung it with such force into the earth that it lay buried fifty fathoms deep.

And hearing the sounds of strife, Amurtsheela hastened to the spot where Sanglun frowned in wrath upon her son, and she cried: "What is amiss, Sanglun? How hath my son offended thee, that thou dost gaze thus darkly upon him?"

And Sanglun made answer: "This is no human child that thou hast borne, but some monster misbegotten of a fiend. Rongsa hath told how he slaughtered nine wethers of the flock to make a feast for beggars, and when I would have punished his insolence, he flouted me and cast my scourge fifty fathoms into the earth."

But Amurtsheela cried: "Fie on thee, my husband, for a graceless churl! Was it through skill of thine that the few wretched beasts bestowed upon thee by thy brother Chotong have multiplied like leaves on summer trees? What wethers didst thou have, what steeds, what camels, ere Yoro came to bless them? Nay, had he devoured half their number, thou wouldst do ill to chide him. And yet even now they are not countless. Tell over their tale. It may be thou wilt find the back of Rongsa who brought these tidings more worthy than Yoro's of thy lash!"

And Sanglun told over the tale of his beasts, and saw that none was lacking of all their multitude. And he summoned Rongsa and beat him with the bridle of his steed, crying: "Thou bearer of false tales! Thou lying rogue! Long ere thy coming Yoro kept my herds, and they flourished and increased, till now they cover all the mountainside. But had he slaughtered them as thou hast told, their numbers would have grown less and not greater. Thou hast an envious heart and a spiteful tongue. Keep guard upon them, Rongsa, for shouldst thou clack such mischief another time, they shall be torn out at the very roots."

And Yoro spoke no word, but Shikeer laughed.

And now Sanglun resolved that he would return to the land of his fathers, and he abandoned the place where the three rivers meet, and journeying for nine days, he reached the border of Nulumtala where dwelt his tribesfolk.

And Chotong beheld the snowy yurta and the browsing kine that stretched in endless hordes over the plain, and he galloped thither to find Sanglun sitting before the portal of his yurta with his three sons beside him.

And Chotong cried: "I greet thee, Sanglun! Whence hast thou thy fair yurta and the cattle that spread farther than eye can see on either hand?"

And Yoro answered him: "Thy folly, Chotong, is as the folly of the chip that knows not the rock whence it was hewn, and of the hound forgetful of his master. Because he suffered evil at thy hands who never injured thee, the gods have smiled on thy brother and showered their blessings upon him."

And Chotong cried: "Thou art bold of speech, strange youth, and since it must be that thy spirit matches thy tongue, I will give thee a task. Go to the country of the seven alwins that devour each day the flesh of seven hundred men and beasts. Say that Chotong hath sent thee as a tender

27

morsel for their delight, and take thy mother with thee, that they may feast the more abundantly."

And Yoro answered: "I will do thy task, Chotong."

But Amurtsheela wrung her hands and cried: "What folly is this, my son? I deemed thee ripe in wisdom, yet now thou wouldst journey to the land of the seven alwins, that they may devour thee. Go, if it be thy will, but as for me, I will tarry here, and let the alwins devour whom they may!"

"Nay, mother, for if thou perish at the hands of Chotong, will thy death be sweeter?"

Then Shikeer knelt in supplication before his brother, crying: "I will go with thee, Yoro, whether for death or life. And if for death, we will die together; and if for life, I would live it by thy side."

And Yoro drew him apart, and clasping him to his breast with tears of joy, he cried: "Now by thy words I know thee for my chosen friend and my heart's brother. And I am Gessar Khan, the son of heaven, sent by Buddha to uproot the tenfold evil and restore gladness to the hearts of men. Yet till my fifteenth year be passed, I may reveal myself to none save thee. Therefore, be patient! Abide with Sanglun and guard him from his wicked brother, but have no care for me, for death lies far from my purpose."

And Yoro loaded his mother's goods upon a yak, and journeyed with her to the country of the seven alwins. And there he felled a sapling and fashioned from its wood seven magic wands. And in a mountain cleft he caught seven hares and roasted them, and the wind bore their savor to the nostrils of the seven alwins. And presently they rode into camp, and on his back each alwin bore a hundred mortals and a hundred steeds. And they cried: "What feast is this whose pleasant savor the wind hath borne to our nostrils?" And their voices were as the voices of lions that have hungered overlong.

And Yoro cried: "A feast no god would spurn of mountain hares and broth and sweet black tea. Pray sit and eat, and lay aside against the morrow's need the meal ye bear on your backs."

And the seven alwins did as Yoro bade them and sat them down to the feast. And for seven days they ate and drank without ceasing, yet still the mountain hares lay whole before them and the cauldron brimmed with tea. And when at length they would have mounted their steeds, so heavy were they grown with much eating that the beasts would not bear them but sank beneath their weight to the ground.

And Yoro cried: "Despair not, ye seven alwins, for I will give you steeds to outrun yours as the wind outruns a camel. Bestride these seven wands that I have fashioned of the wood of yonder sapling, and they will soar with you into the skies or pierce the mountains or bear you over the sea to distant shores. Where will ye find horses of blood and bone to do such wonders?"

And the alwins bestrode the seven wands, crying: "Reveal to us your wonders! Soar with us into the skies! Pierce the thick mountains! Bear us to the distant shores of the sea!" And lifting their heads, the seven wands soared upward and passed over flowering plains and shining rivers.

And when they reached the mountains, they pierced the rock and issued forth beyond, and at length they came to the distant shores of the sea.

And the alwins laughed for pleasure in their wands, and said one to the other: "The youth spoke truly, and these slender wands excel our steeds as the wind excels a camel. But now, having spanned the earth, let us cross the waters. Into the ocean, ye wondrous chargers!"

And leaping into the ocean, the seven wands swam to where its depth cannot be fathomed, and there they hurled the alwins from their backs, and they sank for seven days and seven nights into the dungeons of the dragon-princes who took them captive. But the wands returned to Yoro and bowed before him, in token that their task had been completed. And loading his mother's goods upon a yak and driving before him the mighty steeds he had taken from the alwins, Yoro set forth for home with Amurtsheela.

And when they came to the yurta of Chotong, they found a goodly company assembled to honor the troth of Altantu, his eldest son, with the Lady Kimsun. And the feast was spread, and on one side the lords regaled themselves, and on one side the ladies. And Chotong sat on his throne and ate of the forequarter of a sheep.

But none gave welcome to Amurtsheela and none to Yoro, wherefore they sat them down on the earth, he amid the lords and she amid the ladies, to await what should befall. And the board was laden with all manner of pleasant foods, and the wine flowed freely, yet neither food nor wine was proffered to the lips of the wayfarers.

And at length Yoro cried: "Chotong! My uncle! A mountain of meat lies here and a river of wine! My happy eyes may behold them but my unhappy gullet may not savor them! Chotong, I hunger! Give me of the forequarter clutched in thy hand!"

And Chotong answered: "I would give thee of the left shoulder, Yoro, save that it is the symbol of my fortune! Or the right loin save that it is a charm to shield my daughters! And were I to give thee the forequarter clutched in my hand, the evil of all evils would overtake me and I should be undone. Yet I would not have thee utterly bereft, wherefore, my Yoro, take for thyself the tears of those that weep and the weariness of those that toil and die, and the curse of the barren land that yields no fruit, and the carcasses of beasts dead of the plague. And if these things suffice thee not, good nephew, then take sorrow and take venom and take death!"

And Chotong released a wasp from his nostril and whispered in her ear: "Enter the nostril of mine enemy and, creeping upward till thou find his brain, pierce it with thy deadly fang!"

But when the wasp would have entered Yoro's nostril to pierce his brain, he fixed on her his eye that looked askance, and she quailed before him, venturing neither to the right nor to the left. And Yoro seized her and held her fast in his hand.

And straightway Chotong fell down from his throne and lay upon the ground, as one that had been stricken by the hand of death. But when Yoro loosed his hold upon the wasp, he rose up again and bowed at Yoro's feet. And so he fell and rose and fell again, as Yoro crushed the wasp against his palm or suffered her to breathe.

And Altantu, knowing that his father's soul lay hidden in the wasp, bade the Lady Kimsun plead with Yoro to spare his life. And she knelt before him, proffering in one hand a turquoise huge as the head of an eagle, and in the other hand a skin of wine.

But Yoro frowned upon her and cried: "What forward wench is this that kneels before me? Ever it hath been the custom in Tibet that whoso weds with the son of a great prince should veil her countenance for three years and a day from the gaze of all save her kinsmen. Yea, even she that weds with a humble man will hold herself from sight for three full moons. Yet here is one, pledged to the son of Chotong, that bares her face to me on her bridal day. Is this wasp that I hold captive perchance thy husband or thy father or thy mother, that thou dost sue thus shamelessly for her life?" And with these words, Yoro turned his back upon her.

Then Altantu prostrated himself, crying: "Yoro! Kind Yoro! God-protected Yoro! hear the curse that I lay upon thine enemies! Whoso, beholding thee, denies thee bread, may his eyes be blinded! Who hears thee sue for drink and heeds thee not, may his ears be deafened! Who eats and will not give thee of his food, may his teeth rot in his head! And whoso with a sheep in his right hand proffers thee none, may his right hand be shattered! And now I pray thee, Yoro, release the wasp, and thou shalt wed with the Lady Kimsun!"

32

And Yoro answered: "I may not wed with the Lady Kimsun, but she shall be the bride of my brother Shikeer, if she pleases him."

And Yoro loosed his hold upon the wasp, so that she fluttered in his hand, and he spoke to Chotong, saying: "Arise and bow down before my mother whom thou hast wronged, and entreat her pardon."

And Chotong bowed thrice before Amurtsheela, entreating her pardon, and laid his brow upon her feet.

And Yoro released the wasp and she entered into the nostril of Chotong. And he bore himself arrogantly as of yore, yet he dared not molest his brother Sanglun nor Amurtsheela, for he feared the power of Yoro.

II. YORO REVEALS HIMSELF AS GESSAR KHAN

OF THE WOOING OF THE LADY ROGMO, WHEREIN YORO PROVED HIMSELF MOST DAUNTLESS AMONG HEROES, AND HOW IN THE END HE REVEALED HIMSELF AS GESSAR KHAN.

Now there dwelt in a pleasant land that bordered on Tibet the Lady Rogmo, and she was daughter to Sengeslu Khan, and so radiant was her beauty that of all the princes of her father's tribe, none was deemed worthy to be her mate.

And she sought audience of Sengeslu Khan and said to him: "I will journey to the land of Tibet and seek me there a mate, for men say it is a land peopled by heroes and the sons of gods."

. And she journeyed to the land of Tibet, and a wise lama rode at her right hand, and a princely retinue followed after her, and at her left hand rode three peerless archers and three valiant knights that were her champions.

And in Tibet ten thousand chieftains were gathered to welcome her, and she rode into their midst and cried: "Lords of Tibet! I am come to choose a husband from among you, for men say your land is peopled by heroes and the sons of gods. And that ye may know me worthy to wed with the noblest, I will reveal to you the wonders that marked my birth. Though the skies grew black with clouds, the sun shone brightly among them, yet when they vanished and the heavens cleared, out of the clear heavens the rains poured down. A unicorn and a blue elephant paced round and round about my father's dwelling, and a cuckoo sang above my mother's head, while on her right hand perched a parakeet and on her left a bird without a name. These are the signs of wonder that marked my birth, and therefore am I come among you to seek the hero destined to wed with the Lady Rogmo.

"Six champions bear me company—three warriors whom the mightiest princes of our tribe have sought in vain to overthrow, three bowmen whose skill is such that when they have shot their arrows from the bow, a man may thrice brew tea to slake his thirst ere they return again. More-

38

over, so truly do they aim that each one marks the spot where the arrow should return by laying his head upon it, and only when the arrow plunges earthward does he turn his head aside to make place for it. Such marksmanship as this do my champions boast, and he that would wed with me must still excel it."

And having spoken, Rogmo galloped to the crest of a high hill that overlooked the field, and saw how the lords and princes of Tibet strove with her archers and her warriors and strove in vain. And she cried in scorn: "Though ye be heroes and the sons of gods, yet ye are powerless to overthrow my champions!"

Then Yoro plucked the sleeve of the wise lama that rode at her right hand, and he cried: "I too would strive with Rogmo's champions, for though I be unseemly, my strength is as great as another's."

And the wise lama answered: "Beware, my son, nor venture thy tender bones where mighty warriors have striven in vain."

"Nay, though my bones be shattered into dust, still would I venture, father."

"Then have thy way and may Buddha be thy shield!"

And Yoro's blessèd sisters, seeing his need, lifted him from the earth and set one foot upon a mountain top and one on the shore of the sea. And stooping, Yoro seized the strongest of Lady Rogmo's warriors and hurled him over his head. And the distance that he hurled him was a thousand leagues. And the second he hurled two thousand leagues behind him, and the third and weakest, three thousand. And the people gazed in wonder upon Yoro who had wrought this deed.

And now he stood beside the archers of the Lady Rogmo. And when she gave the signal, each one let fly his arrow, then flung himself upon the ground to await its coming. And at midday three arrows returned from their flight and plunged themselves where lately the heads of the three archers had lain. But the dart of Yoro returned not, for his sisters held it on Sumeru, decking the shaft with gaily plumaged birds to be a sign to Yoro of their love.

And when at length they hurled it earthward, the birds spread wide their wings and hid the sun, so that darkness fell upon the face of the earth and men cried out: "The gods are wroth! Disaster is upon us!" and would have fled in terror.

But Shikeer lifted up his voice above the clamor and cried: "Peace, foolish ones! It is the dart of Yoro that returns from its far flight!"

And the singing shaft plunged itself into the earth where Yoro's head had rested, and the gaily plumaged birds hovered above him, then soared, still singing, into the blue heavens.

And the tribesmen shouted: "Hail to thee, Yoro, defender of the valor of Tibet!"

And Chotong and the great ones that had been vanquished murmured one to another: "Yea, though he be a stripling and ill-favored, with eyes that look askance, yet he hath won the Lady Rogmo for his bride."

And Rogmo descended from the crest of the high hill

and looked upon the ill-favored one that claimed her hand. And she would have turned away in displeasure, but Shikeer held her fast. And he spoke, saying: "Thou art fair, Rogmo, but thou art a woman. And though he be ill-favored as any goat, yet Yoro is a man. Therefore, submit thyself as woman should. Nor be so soon forgetful of thy pledge to wed with him that should encounter thy champions and vanquish them!"

And Rogmo could not choose but yield her hand to Yoro. And with a blade he pricked his finger, and through her red lips Rogmo drew the blood forth from his wound. Then plucking from the tail of a steed three hairs, he wove them together and clasped them about her throat, crying aloud: "Thus do I plight my troth with thee, I, Yoro, with thee, the daughter of Sengeslu Khan!" And they were plighted in the eyes of men.

But when night fell and the encampment slept, Rogmo stole forth from her tent and roused her retinue, and they took horse and galloped swiftly toward her father's realm. And as they sped away, Rogmo cried out: "Who follows after us?"

And the lama turned and viewed the plain and answered: "Naught save the wind!"

And they journeyed farther and again the Lady Rogmo cried: "Who follows after us?"

And the lama turned again and answered: "Naught save the silver shadow of the moon!"

And they journeyed farther, and the Lady Rogmo cried: "Nay, it is neither the wind's breath nor the shadow of the moon that lies upon my cheek! I pray thee, look again!"

And the lama looked and saw that Yoro, cloaked in darkness, sat behind her and clasped her in his arms. And he cried: "He that hath won thee for his wife sits behind thee now and clasps thee in his arms!"

And Rogmo wept and beat her breast, crying: "How shall I hide my shame? I that have spurned great lords and noble khans, how shall I bring my father this offspring of a camel to be his son? Alas, alas, I am lost beyond all hope!" And thus lamenting, she continued on her way, and Yoro sat behind her, but spoke no word.

And when they were come within a hundred leagues of her father's kingdom, he caused a cloud of dust to rise before them as from the hoofbeats of ten thousand steeds, and the great Sengeslu Khan, watching from afar, turned to his councillors and cried: "It must be that our daughter is fallen to the lot of China's glorious Khan!"

And now the cloud of dust grew less, as though a thousand chargers, fleet of foot, drove it before them. And the joy of Sengeslu Khan was abated and he cried: "Though she hath missed the mightiest, yet she returns the bride of some great lord whose name will be to us a crown of glory."

And ever the cloud of dust grew less, till it was grown so small that it might be the herald of scarce a hundred swiftly flying steeds. And the brow of Sengeslu Khan grew black with foreboding, but he took heart again, crying: "Chotong, a prince of fair repute, hath won my daughter."

And now, surrounded by his chieftains, he made ready to welcome the Lady Rogmo and him that she had chosen from all the world to be her worthy mate. And the cavalcade approached his yurta, and his daughter alighted from her steed and bowed before him, weeping bitterly. And Yoro followed after her.

And her father looked upon him and cried: "Is this the hero thou hast sought through the broad earth? Is this the god that hath subdued thine arrogance? Truly, my daughter, thou hast chosen a strange husband, and there is none that will dispute thy choice with thee. Only beware lest the hounds howling at night mistake him not for an abandoned carcass and so devour him!" And turning his back upon them, he entered into his yurta, but his knights encircled Yoro and taunted him, prodding him with their spears.

Now in Tibet Chotong arose at dawn, and saw that Yoro was vanished from among them, neither could he discover trace of Rogmo nor her princely retinue. And he was filled with spleen, and summoned the great ones of the tribe and said to them: "Kinsmen and brothers! Dishonor and shame shall be your portion, if ye sit idly by and suffer a beggar to enjoy the prize that should have been a prince's. Through guile and treachery hath Yoro won the Lady Rogmo, and not in equal combat. Wherefore let us go forth and succor her from an unworthy mate!"

And he gave spurs to his steed, and galloped over the plain, and all the nobles of his tribe galloped behind him until at length they reached the kingdom of Sengeslu Khan.

And they halted before his abode, and he came forth amid his councillors and spoke to them, saying: "Whence

44

do ye come, men of an alien land, and what is your will with me?"

And they answered: "We come from far Tibet, where Yoro strove against thy daughter's champions and overthrew them. And we would have thee yield her up to us, for Yoro is unworthy to be her mate."

"And though he be unworthy, how shall I take her from him, since he hath met her challenge and overthrown her champions?"

"We are not come to reason with thee, old man, but to hear thy yea or nay. If thou deem Yoro too poor a thing to wed with thy daughter, then yield her up to us. But if thou art fain to cling to this treasure thou hast won, know that the princes of Tibet have wrought destruction upon heads nobler than thine."

And Sengeslu Khan, being a just monarch and a righteous, yet fearful of the loud-tongued strangers that menaced him, knew not how he should reply to them. And he went apart with his ministers, and they took council together, and presently he returned to the princes of Tibet and his answer was in his mouth.

"Fierce words have ye spoken, warriors from afar, and patiently have I heard you. Hear ye now me. In marksmanship and in the art of single combat Yoro hath shown himself your master. Yet he is graceless and mean of stature and ill-fitted to wed with the Lady Rogmo. Therefore do I decree a match among you, and he whose steed shall first bear him to the appointed goal, shall take the Lady Rogmo

45

to wife. But if my decree offend you, then let us wage war upon one another, for none shall persuade me from this course."

And Chotong answered: "Let it be as thou hast decreed."

And the edict went forth, and thirty thousand men gathered to contend for the hand of the Lady Rogmo. And Yoro scattered incense and offered up a sacrifice to Kormuzda, crying: "My father and father of the gods! Let the brown wonder-steed descend, for I have need of him!"

And Kormuzda answered: "He will descend, my son, yet not in splendor as thou hast known him, but as a shrunken foal of two years' growth. For it is not meet that thou shouldst ride a godlike steed till thou have revealed thyself as Gessar Khan!"

And when he had spoken, a whirlwind descended out of the heavens, invisible to all save Yoro, and when it touched the earth a shrunken foal of two years' growth stepped forth, and circled round and round, seeking his master. And when he espied Yoro, he bowed before him and stood quietly.

And Yoro clambered upon his back and rode into the company of heroes, and when they beheld him astride his shrunken steed, they flung back their heads and mighty laughter shook them.

But Sengeslu Khan spoke sternly to Yoro, saying: "Dost thou hope with this beast, unsightly as thyself, to overtake the proud steeds of thy rivals? Or is it thy purpose to affront my daughter, unhappy that she is? Go take a stallion from my herds, swift-paced and ardent, and leave this stunted foal, lest thou shame me beyond all measure in the sight of men."

And Yoro answered: "I will not take thy stallion, swift-paced and ardent, but on my stunted foal I will run this match and abide the issue."

And Sengeslu Khan raised his hand aloft, signalling the departure, and thirty thousand riders leaped forward and vanished from sight. But Yoro, restraining his heavenly steed, was left behind till presently he loosed his hold upon him, and the brown wonder-steed in a single bound overtook ten thousand horsemen. And again he curbed him and again he set him free, and with a single bound he overtook again ten thousand horsemen. And yet a third time Yoro held him in check, then let him go his way, and now he had overtaken all save the blue-black steed of Chotong.

And Yoro said to him: "My little wonder-steed of two years' growth that in three bounds hath overtaken the glory of Tibet, when thou art come close to the blue-black steed of Chotong, do thou smite him with thy forefeet and tumble steed and rider into the dust."

And the foal did as Yoro bade him, and with his forefeet smote the blue-black steed of Chotong and overthrew him. And Chotong rolled in the dust, crying: "Alas, Yoro, what hast thou done to me?"

And Yoro answered: "Alas, uncle, I know not, for I seek but to safeguard my treasure from thieves that would despoil me, and thy blue-black steed hath barred my way." So saying, he galloped past him and reached the goal.

And Sengeslu Khan proclaimed: "Yoro hath won my daughter a second time."

But the princes of Tibet murmured together and they went before Sengeslu Khan and said: "Truly Yoro hath reached the goal before us all, and therefore he may be accounted a skilful horseman. But he that shall slay the Wild Boar of the Wilderness and bring thee for a sign his tail fashioned of thirteen strands, him shalt thou know as a hero, marked of the gods and worthy to wed with the Lady Rogmo."

And Sengeslu Khan decreed that he who slew the Wild Boar of the Wilderness should wed with the Lady Rogmo. And thirty thousand chieftains sallied forth to hunt him, but Yoro was the first to come upon him where he bellowed in the forest, lashing his mighty tail and felling a hundred oaks at every blow. And he took aim and sped his shining arrow swiftly to the Wild Boar's heart and slew him. And as he was about to sever the tail, fashioned of thirteen strands, Chotong espied him and hailed him with honeyed words, crying: "Now is the maiden thine, good nephew, beyond gainsaying, and none shall take her from thee. Therefore, I pray thee, give me the Wild Boar's tail and I will bind it upon the bridle of my steed, and as the herald of thy valor will I bear it before the people, crying: 'Yoro, my kinsman, hath slain the Wild Boar of the Wilderness!' Thus shall I share thy glory, and nevermore will I chide thee or use thee ill, but I will cherish thee more tenderly than the children of my loins."

"Take thou the tail, good uncle, for it is naught to me!"

And Yoro severed the tail from the Wild Boar's body and gave it to Chotong, yet gave him not the whole, having thrust secretly into his bosom three strands thereof.

And Chotong galloped joyfully to the meeting-place, crying: "Comrades and heroes! Leave ye the hunt and pursue the chase no longer! For I, Chotong of Lik, have slain the Wild Boar of the Wilderness. I have bound his tail, fashioned of thirteen strands, to the bridle of my stallion, and I claim the Lady Rogmo for my wife."

But Yoro who followed behind him cried: "Alack, thou faithless one, didst thou not come to me when I had slain the Boar and pray that I might give thee the tail? Didst thou not say: 'I will proclaim thee victor and share thy glory'?"

"What villainy is this, thou wry-eyed knave? Dost thou think with railing and false oaths to wrest from me again what I have taken?"

"Sayest thou so, Chotong? Then show me this tail, fashioned of thirteen strands, that thou didst take from the Wild Boar to be a sign of thy victory?"

And Chotong drew forth the tail and held it aloft in triumph, but soon his joy was turned to dismay, for he saw that the tail, fashioned of thirteen strands, bore only ten and that three strands were lacking.

And Yoro cried: "Did I not know thee for a shameless liar, and did I not therefore withhold from thee three strands of the mighty tail when in the forest thou didst entreat me to give it thee?" And with these words Yoro drew from his bosom the strands that had been lacking. And Chotong was shamed before the multitude and, turning his steed, galloped in haste away.

But now there rode out of the wilderness a horseman whose steed was flecked with foam, and his eyes shone like the eyes of one that hath looked on a god, and his lips bore tidings of wonder. And he cried out: "My lords and princes, following through the wilderness the Wild Boar's track, I heard the song of the Garuda Bird. And gazing upward, I beheld her where she sat in a tall pine, preening her golden plumage."

And Sengeslu Khan commanded his soothsayer to come before him and cried: "Read me this omen!"

And the soothsayer read the omen and answered: "It is the voice of heaven that bids thee give thy daughter to him that shall pluck from the tail of the magic bird her golden plumage, for none may pluck it forth save by the will of the high gods."

And Sengeslu Khan made known the word of the soothsayer to the heroes assembled before him, and they rode into the wilderness to try if they might pluck from the tail of the Garuda Bird her golden plumage.

And Yoro remained behind for a brief space, then followed after them, and when he came upon them, they were gathered together at the foot of a tall pine, and their arrows beat about the head of the Garuda Bird like silver rain. But she sat upon the topmost branch, unheeding of their darts, and uttered her strange cry and preened the golden plumage of her tail.

And Yoro spoke unto her soft words of praise, saying:

51

"Proud bird! How sweetly soars thy voice above all others in this wilderness! Even so, I ween, does thy bright plumage outshine the plumage of thy lesser brethren! Would we might gaze upon thee in thy glory!"

And the breast of the Garuda Bird grew big with pride, and she walked forth upon the branch that all might gaze on her, and she lifted her mighty pinions and let them fall again, and turned her stately head now to this side and now to that, flaunting her beauty.

And Yoro cried: "In truth, thy radiance is as the sun breaking through storm-clouds. But what of thy flight, O gracious bird of heaven, for surely when thy pinions bear thee above the earth, thou art like some god descended from Sumeru to dazzle with his splendor the eyes of men."

And hearing these words, the magic bird spread wide her wings and floated above the trees serenely as a cloud in a clear sky. But Yoro cried: "Draw nearer, thou blessèd one, that we may bow before thy majesty!" And she drew nearer, and all the multitude were blinded by her beauty and veiled their eyes in dread before her, but Yoro put forth his hand and plucked two golden feathers from her tail. And the Garuda Bird uttered a piercing cry and soared aloft and vanished.

And now Yoro, giving no heed to those that pressed about him, rode to the meeting-place, and the chieftains of Tibet rode hard behind him. And when he was come to where the Lady Rogmo sat among her maidens, he bade her rise, and into her headdress he bound the golden plumes of the Garuda Bird.

And as he did so, the heavens darkened, and the gods, arching their bows, sped shafts of flame to the four corners of the sky, and the voices of their dragon-steeds thundered across the blackness, and from the everlasting streams the waters of life were loosed upon the multitude, beating them to the earth. And loud above the din a cry rang forth: "The gods have triumphed! Evil is put to rout!"

And when the darkness lifted and the floods ceased, a wonder stood revealed. For there where Yoro had sat astride his shrunken foal, a warrior, mounted on a lordly steed, towered above them. And his countenance was as the countenance of one beloved of Buddha, and his breast was as the breast of the mountain gods, and his thighs were as the thighs of the dragon-princes that dwell beneath the sea. And his armor was fashioned of seven jewels that sparkled like the dew at dawn, and a helmet, wrought of the woven light of the sun and moon, decked his noble head. And by his side he bore a lightning-sword three fathoms long, and an ebon bow was girded about his shoulders, and from his quiver thirty silver arrows, turquoise-notched, raised their bright heads.

And Shikeer, arrayed in splendor, was mounted beside him and thirty shining heroes surrounded him.

And the warrior lifted up his voice and cried: "Ye heedless ones! Ye men of little worth! Know me for Gessar Khan, the son of heaven, sent by almighty Buddha to be your lord, that the tenfold evil may be uprooted and gladness restored to the hearts of men! Full fifteen years have I dwelt among you in Yoro's guise, for thus hath it been decreed. Yet when I journeyed into the country of the seven alwins and drove them beneath the sea, did I not reveal myself as a doer of mighty deeds? And when I seized in my hand the soul of Chotong and was like to destroy him, could ye not see in me one that had been marked of the gods? And when, with one foot on the mountaintop and one on the shore of the sea, I hurled the warriors of the Lady Rogmo over my head; and when I vanquished her archers and my arrow returned from the skies decked with birds of gay plumage; and when on a stunted foal of two years' growth I overtook the chargers of thrice ten thousand men, reaching the goal before them; and when I slew the Wild Boar of the Wilderness and plucked two golden feathers from the tail of the Garuda Bird, ye blind, ye sinful ones, though I was graceless and mean of stature, with eyes that looked askance, were these wondrous signs and portents no more to you than snowfall in winter or the braying of a wild ass on the mountainside?

"Bow down before me, for I am Kormuzda's son!

"Bow down before me, for I am the servant of Buddha!

"Bow down before me, ye princes and tribesmen and beggars, for I am the light of your darkness, the food of your hunger and the scourge of your evildoing! I wield the sword of righteousness in one hand! Let my foes beware of its edge! I bear the balm of peace in the other! Let my friends savor its sweetness! The lama of lamas is come to judge among you! Bow down before him! The prince of warriors is come to lead you to battle! Bow down before him! The all-conquering, all-healing Gessar Khan is come

54

to dwell in your midst! Bow down before him, ye men of earth, and pay him homage!"

And all the people bowed down before him in awe and wonder.

And the Lady Rogmo was first to raise her head. And when she beheld the glory of Gessar Khan, she laughed aloud and then she wept for joy.

III. THE JOURNEY TO CHINA

O F GESSAR KHAN'S JOURNEY TO CHINA, WHERE
HE RESTORED PEACE TO KEEME KHAN AND
HIS TROUBLED KINGDOM AND HOW HE WAS
AIDED THEREIN BY A BALDHEADED SMITH.

Now it chanced that the fair **wife** of China's lord, the
noble Keeme Khan, sickened and died. And so great was
his grief that he would not be comforted, but sent his criers
forth into the land to proclaim his word:

"Disaster is our portion and woe our lot! Therefore

let him that hears the tidings of sorrow as he journeys, journey forever, mourning the khanin. Let him that bides at home mourn her at home, nor cross again the threshold of his dwelling! Let him that feasts still feast and weep for her, and he that fasts, let him not cease from fasting and lamentation. Thus shall the khanin's memory be honored, nor perish from our hearts!" And the Khan sat upon his throne and held to his breast her body, whose spirit was departed to the dread kingdom of Erleek Khan.

But his edict was hateful to the people, and they muttered against him, yielding with an ill grace to his command. And in the end his ministers assembled in council, and he that was chief among them rose up and said:

"My lords, the khanin is dead. Fitting it were that her body be delivered to the flames, and that the holy lamas of our land read Buddha's word for nine and forty days above her ashes. Moreover, alms should be scattered and bounty freely showered on all in want, the dowerless and the beggar. Then let the Khan array his body in bridal garments and take unto himself another wife, that he may minister unto the needs of his people and rejoice their hearts. For is this khanin the first that Erleek Khan hath summoned to his dread kingdom? And is there one of us that shall not follow her hereafter? Verily, madness hath laid hold upon our Khan and folly counsels him, and if ye know the man that will comfort his grief and lead his spirit back to sweet reason, I pray you name him to me."

But none could name the man, though for long hours they held counsel with one another.

Now there dwelt in the court of Keeme Khan a smith, skilled in his craft, but meddlesome and of a prattling tongue, and ever his bald head was thrust where the great gathered. And learning what was afoot, he stood now at the door of the council-chamber and hearkened to those within. Then, having heard his fill, he hastened homeward, and his goodwife met him upon the threshold of their hut.

And he said to her: "The wits of these ministers move nimbly as an ailing elephant. All day they wrangle, and still they cannot name the man who may bring comfort to the soul of Keeme Khan. Yet I—a humble smith—I know that none save the all-healing Gessar Khan, lord of the ten great regions of the earth and Buddha's messenger, hath power to solace him."

And his goodwife answered: "Thou sinful baldhead! Thou fellow of little worth! Where the sages of the Khan are unknowing, thou wouldst be wise! They falter, but thou art firm-footed as a wild ass before a precipice that will not see the perils awaiting him! Go to thy forge, thou bearer of idle tales, and hold thy peace!"

But when the smith saw that she would not suffer him to do his will, he feigned great anger and cried: "Rash woman, meddle not with me, but set about thy duties! My paunch is hollow as a kettledrum, yet no fire is laid nor no meal prepared to feed my hunger. Fetch water from the stream and curb thy railing tongue, else shalt thou feel my staff about thy shoulders!"

And she went to fetch water from the stream, but the smith hied him again unto the council-chamber, and sought an audience. And the chief minister bade him enter and said: "What is thy suit?"

"My lords and ministers! Have ye found him that shall bring healing to the soul of Keeme Khan?"

"We have not found him. Canst thou name him to us?"

"That can I. The mighty Gessar Khan, lord of the ten great regions of the earth, and Buddha's messenger, he only hath power to do this deed."

"Thy words are just, yet he dwells in a far country, and who will move him to journey hither that he may serve our need? Wilt thou essay the task?"

"Right gladly, if ye will give me a steed to bear me, and a companion to lighten my way."

And they gave him a swift steed, and a companion to lighten his way, and he set forth and journeyed for many moons until he reached the mountains of Tibet and the shining yurta of Gessar Khan.

Now Gessar had knowledge of this smith and of his errand, and when he came into his presence, the son of heaven fixed upon him a glance so baleful that the smith quaked in terror, and his limbs would not bend beneath him nor bear him upright, and he could move neither forward nor back nor bow in greeting, but only stood agape at Gessar Khan.

And Gessar cried: "Why, what a blundering baldhead is this that seeks my presence! Canst thou not move nor sit nor bow to me in greeting? Wilt thou stand thus forever and shake thy knees, like grain in a high wind? Whence art thou? Why dost thou come before me?"

But still the smith could utter no word and Gessar, taking pity upon him, removed his baleful glance and eyed him in friendliness. Then only did the smith regain his wits, and he bowed down in greeting and said: "Dread son of heaven! The wife of China's noble lord is departed to the kingdom of Erleek Khan! And so great is his grief that he will not give her body to be delivered to the flames, but sits upon his throne, clasping her to his breast. Moreover, he hath proclaimed: 'Let every man that journeys journey forever, mourning the khanin! Let him that bides at home mourn her at home, nor cross again the threshold of his dwelling! Let him that feasts still feast and weep for her, and he that fasts, let him not cease from fasting and lamentation! Thus shall the khanin's memory be honored, nor perish from our hearts!' Now this edict is the edict of a fool, and not of a wise khan. Wherefore the people mutter against him, and the ministers have sent me hither, that I might entreat thee to comfort the soul of our master and lead his spirit back to sweet reason, for well they know that none save the all-healing Gessar Khan hath power to do this deed."

"What! Is it for this that I am come among you—to solace grieving khans who set their will above the will of the gods? Is this my mission?"

"I know not, master. Yet if thou deny us, there is no help beneath the heavens nor above the earth."

"I know thee, smith, for one skilled in thy craft, but meddlesome and of a prattling tongue, and ever fain to thrust thy head where the great gather. Not to bring succor to thy

63

Khan didst thou come hither, but that thy fellows might account thee a man of mark. So prove it then. For this task that thou hast proffered me, I stand in need of three treasures—a stag's horn filled with blood from the beak of an eagle, a goat's horn filled with milk from the breast of his mate, a sheep's horn filled with tears from the eyes of his fledgling. Bring me these treasures and I will journey with thee to distant China, to solace thy Khan and to restore peace to his kingdom. But if thou bring them not after three days, thou shalt be cast into a seething cauldron, and thy flesh shall be flung to the vultures, and of thy kull a goblet shall be wrought for the least of my household."

And the smith went forth from the presence of Gessar Khan, and he was sore afflicted, for he knew not how he should accomplish his task. And for two days he clambered about the mountains and scanned the skies, casting his snare in vain. And he wept and cried: "Would I were safe within my lowly hut! Nevermore should I seek the councils of the mighty, but bide at home, toiling from dawn to dusk and heeding the prudent words of my goodwife!"

And as he spoke, sleep came to him, and she led a dream by the hand, and the dream said: "Go to the mouth of the river Nyrandsa, and where thou shalt find the carrion of a cow, there cast thy snare, and delve a pit and hide thyself within. Then will that come to pass which hath been foretold."

And the smith awoke. And he went to the mouth of the river Nyrandsa, and where he found the carrion of a cow,

he cast his snare, and delved a pit and laid himself within, awaiting what should befall.

And presently a black eagle flew out of the north, and his mate flew after him, and behind them their fledgling followed. And the black eagle circled above the carrion, and spoke to his mate, and said: "I will go down and eat my fill of the carrion, for none is by to hinder me."

But his mate replied: "Go not, my love. For it is unseemly that a bird of the heavens should descend to eat of the foul flesh that rots on earth—monstrous indeed, as though some earthbound creature should soar aloft to share the skies with us. I pray thee, go not."

"Nay, I will go warily, peering on every hand. And if no creature stirs, I will tarry and eat, for the flesh of this carrion is tender beyond my dreams. Yet should I mark so much as a reed's trembling, I will return straightway."

And he descended, peering on every hand, but he marked not so much as a reed's trembling. Wherefore he alighted upon the carrion and ate, and so sweet was the savor of the flesh that he ceased not from eating, until he came at length to the breast. Then did the smith leap forth out of the pit, and drawing fast the threads of his snare, he captured the black eagle.

And the eagle beat his wings in frenzy and smote his beak against his captor's staff, so that blood flowed out of the wound. And the smith gathered the blood in a stag's horn, and laid it within his scrip.

But now the eagle's mate drew nigh with piteous plaints,

and hovered above his head and cried: "Alas, my husband! Did I not bid thee beware of peril? Now must thou eat of the bitter fruit of thy rashness, and perish in misery."

But the smith cried: "Not so, thou eagle's mate! For have I harmed thy husband? And for the blood I have taken from his beak, it is but a little blood and soon renewed. Say, wouldst thou save him from death?"

"Yea, master."

"Then fill me full this goat's horn with thy milk, and in this sheep's horn gather thy fledgling's tears, and when thou hast brought them to me, I will release him." And the smith loosed the threads of his snare, and suffered the black eagle to lift his head and flutter his prisoned wings, then drew them fast again.

And the eagle's mate took from the smith the goat's horn and the sheep's horn, and the one she filled with milk from her breast, then chid her fledgling till he wept bitterly, and in the other gathered his tears. These she brought to the smith, who took them and released the black eagle, and the three soared into the blue heavens and vanished.

And now the smith returned to Gessar Khan and bowed in greeting. And Gessar said: "What of thy quest, bald-headed smith?"

And the smith answered: "The quest is ended, lord." And from his scrip he took the stag's horn and the goat's horn and the sheep's horn, and proffered them to Gessar.

And Gessar took them and said: "Thou hast done my bidding, and I will journey with thee to China to solace thy

67

Khan and restore peace to thy kingdom." So they set forth, and the smith rode beside the mighty Gessar Khan, but his companion rode behind them.

And when they came to distant China, they dismounted before the palace of Keeme Khan, and Gessar entered in. And he passed through many chambers until he reached a hall of marble columns, whose casements were of bronze, and in each casement a crystal was set, that the golden light of the sun might enter in. And the ceiling was of silver and of ivory, and the walls were jewels that gleamed softly like the embers of a flame. And on his throne, that had been carved out of an emerald, sat Keeme Khan, and held the body of his khanin in his arms.

And Gessar said: "Ill-omened is that dwelling, O Khan, wherein the quick consort with the dead. Therefore do as thy fathers did before thee, and deliver up to the flames her body whose spirit is departed to the kingdom of Erleek Khan. And let the lamas assemble to perform above her ashes the holy rites, and let bounty be scattered among the needy. When this is done, take thou another wife, for it is not meet that a Khan so mighty nor an empire so glorious as thine should lack a sovereign lady."

But Keeme answered: "This fellow babbles madness, for neither after one year nor after ten will I put my wife from my arms."

And Gessar went forth from the hall of columns, and the ministers of the Khan bowed down before him, and cried: "Dread son of heaven! Glorious Gessar Khan! Hast thou brought our master healing?"

68

And he answered: "Thy master's soul is sick unto death and none can heal him."

But when night fell and Keeme Khan slept on his throne, Gessar stole secretly into the hall of columns, and took the body of the khanin from his arms, and left an ape therein. And the sentinel that stood watch over the Khan would have cried the alarm, but his tongue clave to the roof of his mouth, and no sound came forth.

And with the dawn Keeme Khan awoke, and the ape danced in his arms. But he flung it from him, crying: "Woe! Woe is me! Grievously have I offended against the gods, and they have punished me, transforming my wife into an ape."

But now the tongue of the sentinel was loosed, and he prostrated himself before his master and cried: "Nay, mighty lord! He that men call the son of heaven, noble Gessar Khan, stole hither in the night and took from thine arms the body of the khanin and left the ape therein. And though I strove to cry the alarm, I could not, for my tongue clave to the roof of my mouth, and no sound came forth. Wherefore thy servant hath merited death at thy hands, O dispenser of justice!"

"Nay, not thou shalt die, but he that hath done this deed! Let him be cast into the Hole of Wasps, that they may pierce his eyes from his head and harry him to death."

And Gessar was cast into the Hole of Wasps. But when they swarmed about him and would have pierced his eyes from his head, he scattered the tears of the black fledgling among them and the wasps breathed their odor and perished.

And Gessar slept, but with the dawn he lifted up his voice and sang: "The glorious Khan of China thought to slay me by casting me into his Hole of Wasps. Yet he must needs rejoice in the end that Gessar was not slain by his wasps, but his wasps by Gessar."

And the Keeper of the Hole of Wasps betook himself to Keeme Khan, and reported the words of Gessar. And the Khan frowned and cried: "Let him be cast into the Pit of Serpents, that they may dart their venom into his body and so destroy him."

And Gessar was cast into the Pit of Serpents, but when they would have darted their venom into his body, he scattered the milk of the black eagle's mate among them, and they breathed its odor and perished. And he strewed them about the ground, that they might be a couch for his limbs, and the greatest he laid beneath his head for a soft pillow.

And so he slept. But with the dawn he lifted up his voice and sang: "The illustrious Khan of China sought to slay me by casting me into his Pit of Serpents. Yet he must needs rejoice in the end that Gessar was not slain by his serpents, but his serpents by Gessar."

And the Keeper of the Pit of Serpents hastened to Keeme Khan, and reported the words of Gessar. And the Khan's brow darkened in wrath, and he thundered: "Let this blasphemer be cast into the Den of Wild Beasts, that they may rend his limbs asunder and devour his flesh to the last morsel."

And Gessar was cast forthwith into the Den of Wild Beasts, but when they would have fallen upon him to rend

70

his limbs asunder, he scattered the blood of the black eagle among them, and they breathed its odor and perished. And from the mightiest tiger he stripped the skin, and fashioned a saddle for his brown wonder-steed.

And when the dawn broke, Gessar lifted up his voice and sang: "The exalted Khan of China sought to slay me by casting me into his Den of Wild Beasts. Yet he must needs rejoice in the end that Gessar was not slain by his wild beasts, but his wild beasts by Gessar."

And the Keeper of the Den of Wild Beasts fled trembling to the palace, and reported to Keeme Khan the words of Gessar. And the Khan rose up from his throne and in his countenance a storm raged.

And he cried: "Let this doer of evil and speaker of idle words be brought unto the ramparts, where four and twenty spearsmen shall mete out to him the vengeance of the Khan!"

And Gessar was led unto the ramparts. But as he went, a crimson parrot alighted on his hand, and to her leg he made fast a silken thread, a thousand fathoms long, and so slender that it was visible to none save him. And when he came to the ramparts, four and twenty spearsmen surrounded him, and the Khan stood before them to give the signal.

But Gessar lifted high his hand, whereon the crimson parrot was perched, and cried aloud: "Fly swiftly, my parrot, to Tibet, and seek out Shikeer my brother, and my thirty heroes, and the three hundred chieftains of the tribes. And say to them: 'The Khan of China hath foully slain your

72

lord, that Buddha sent to uproot the tenfold evil and bring you peace. March therefore at the head of all your hosts into his kingdom and ravage his green fields, and scatter his people, and put their dwelling places to the torch. And when ye have worked havoc on every hand, do ye contrive for him a shameful death, that his transgression against the gods and against Gessar may be atoned.'"

So saying, he released the parrot, who vanished from sight, but the silken thread he released not, binding it to his wrist.

Now the Khan pondered long on Gessar's words, and the ministers whispered to one another, and in the end he that was chief among them bowed down before his master and spoke.

"O flower of righteousness! Thrice hast thou condemned this Gessar to bitter death, yet not the wasp's sting nor the serpent's fang nor the jaws of the wild beast have availed against him. Surely it is a sign that the gods cherish him above all men, nor will they suffer evil to approach him or those that follow him. How then shall we subdue Shikeer his brother, or his thirty heroes or the three hundred chieftains of his tribe? Rather will their hosts descend upon us and sack thy cities and destroy thy people, leaving behind no trace of all thy glory. Wherefore we pray thee, O thou whose wisdom is as the never-failing mountain stream, bid Gessar recall his parrot, and pledge him in return whatsoever boon lieth nearest his heart."

And Keeme Khan made answer: "Mine ears are open to the prayers of my people. Do thou, lord of the ten great regions of the earth, recall thy parrot, and whatsoever boon lieth nearest thy heart, ask and it shall be granted thee."

But Gessar said, "Alas, thou son and sire of Khans, fain would I do thy will, but this parrot is flown beyond the sound of my calling."

Then did the people fling themselves at the feet of Gessar, loudly entreating him, and Keeme Khan added his voice to theirs.

"I pray thee, noble Gessar, dread son of heaven, chosen of the gods, recall thy parrot, and whatsoever thou shalt command me, that will I do though the Fearful Ones themselves forbid it."

"Wilt thou give the body of thy khanin to the flames, taking unto thyself another spouse?"

"Even as thou sayest."

"Wilt thou give me thy daughter Aralgo, the maiden whom men call Ten Thousand Joys, to be my second wife?"

"That will I also, and count it a blessing on my house."

Then Gessar lifted up his voice and cried: "Fly back, my parrot, for the word I bade thee bear into Tibet is an idle word, and not to be regarded."

And he drew toward him the silken thread a thousand fathoms long, and out of the western sky the crimson parrot flew swiftly toward him, and lighted on his hand.

And Keeme Khan gave the body of his khanin to be delivered to the flames, and for nine and forty days the lamas read the holy word of Buddha above her ashes, and alms were freely scattered among the needy. And the Khan took unto himself another wife. But upon Gessar he bestowed the hand of Aralgo, his daughter, the maiden whom men called Ten Thousand Joys. And a great feast was spread, and in the streets the gongs were sounded and the drums beaten, for the people rejoiced that Gessar had brought healing to the spirit of Keeme Khan. And the baldheaded smith was bidden to the feast, and sat at the left hand of Gessar.

And for the space of three years Gessar dwelt in China with Aralgo, but when that time was spent he said to her: "I have healed thy father's grief, and for three years I have sojourned by thy side in the land of China. Now my heart hungers for my people, and for the Lady Rogmo, appointed of the gods to be my mate. Wherefore I will return into my country, and thou shalt ride with me till we be come to the Valley of Pleasant Winds, that lies the distance of a month's journey from Tibet. There shalt thou dwell on the sunny hillside, and I will give thee copper vessels and household goods and flocks of comely beasts, and vassals to do thy bidding. Over all these treasures shalt thou be mistress, if thou wilt pledge to me thy constant faith."

And Aralgo, the Lady of Ten Thousand Joys, pledged Gessar her constant faith, and they took leave of Keeme Khan and set forth on their way.

And when they came to the Valley of Pleasant Winds, a yurta, fair to behold, stood on the hillside, and flocks of comely beasts grazed in the pastures. And Gessar bade farewell to Aralgo, and journeyed farther.

And presently he came to a high mountain, from whose summit he looked down upon the world. And a great weariness enfolded him, and he cried: "Mighty Kormuzda! I have labored long, and many excellent deeds have I brought to pass for the glory of thy name! Now I am weary and would tarry upon this mountain-top and regard the world."

But his three sisters appeared to him and said: "Belovèd brother! Thy head is as the head of Buddha, thy breast as the breasts of the mountain gods that sit on the four peaks of Sumeru and guard the earth, thy loins are as the loins of the dragon-princes that dwell beneath the sea. Whom thy rod chastises is cleansed of sin, whom thy hand slays is purged of his unrighteousness. Art thou not Gessar Khan, Kormuzda's son, lord of the ten great regions of the earth, and Buddha's servant? What loftier destiny dost thou hope to earn by resting on the summit of this mountain and regarding the world?"

And Gessar said: "My sisters counsel wisely. Not to regard the world did we tarry here, but that we might refresh our weary limbs, I and my wonder-steed." And Gessar went down from the mountain and journeyed farther.

And he sent a dream to the Lady Rogmo, who lay beneath the skin of a sable in her yurta and slept. And the dream said: "My Lady Rogmo! Thy nose lies buried in thy sable skin as the nose of a red calf in a deep meadow. It were more fitting in thee to rise at daybreak, and frolic like a fawn on the mountain peak, for Gessar Khan, thy lord, is close at hand."

And the Lady Rogmo arose, and clothed her body in bright garments, and called to her servant Arigon, and said: "Brave Arigon! thy master and my belovèd lord is close at hand. Hasten, therefore, to prepare sweet tea, that he may slake his thirst and comfort his weariness, for he journeys from afar."

76

But Arigon answered: "Truly, my mistress, thy body is like a jewelled casket, rich in beauty, but thy thoughts are as shreds of rubbish lying within. My body is unlovely as the belly of an ancient steed, yet my thoughts adorn it as with the rarest of silks. Dost thou think to content the mighty Gessar Khan, that returns again to his people after long journeying, with a cauldron of tea? Take shame unto thyself, fair Lady Rogmo, for such a welcome, and learn from me thy duty. Let a swift courier ride to the source of the Lion's Stream, where Sanglun dwells with Amurtsheela, and bear to them the tidings that Gessar is at hand. Let another ride to the Stream of the Elephant, where the Lord Shikeer awaits his brother's coming. Let the thirty heroes be summoned, and the three hundred chieftains of the tribes, that they may greet their master with worthy gifts, and let a feast be spread of roasted oxen and mountain hares and sweet black tea, while cymbals clash and kettledrums are beaten to honor the return of Gessar Khan."

And the Lady Rogmo answered: "Thy words are full of light as the noonday sun. Go thou and order all things even as thou hast unfolded them to me."

And Arigon ordered all things even as he had unfolded them to the Lady Rogmo, and from the Lion's Stream Sanglun came riding with Amurtsheela, and from the Stream of the Elephant galloped the Lord Shikeer, laughing for joy. And the thirty heroes and the three hundred chieftains of the tribes assembled with gifts to greet their master, and a feast was prepared of roasted oxen and mountain hares and sweet black tea, while cymbals clashed and kettledrums

77

were beaten to honor the return of Gessar Khan. And the Lady Rogmo stood at the threshold of her yurta to welcome him.

And he approached on his brown wonder-steed and, dismounting, he embraced the Lady Rogmo and Shikeer his brother, and his mother Amurtsheela and Sanglun. And the thirty heroes and the three hundred chieftains of the tribes proffered him gifts of the skins of beasts, and weapons cunningly wrought, and steeds that were blue as the turquoise and red as the ruby and black as the deepest night.

And so for thirty days they feasted, rejoicing that their lord was come again to dwell in the midst of his people, and in the end they returned to their tribes and habitations, but Gessar abode among them, and ruled them wisely according to the law of Buddha.

78

IV. THE VALLEY OF PLEASANT WINDS

O F HOW CHOTONG WREAKED HIS VENGEANCE
UPON THE LADY ARALGO, AND SHE WAS
DRIVEN FORTH AND SOUGHT SHELTER IN
THE COUNTRY OF THE TWELVE-HEADED GIANT.

Now Aralgo, the Lady of Ten Thousand Joys, dwelt in
the Valley of Pleasant Winds that lay the distance of a
month's journey from Tibet. And the wily Chotong learned
of her hiding place and, mounting his russet mare, he journeyed thither, and came upon her where she stood at the
threshold of her yurta, eyeing her flocks.

And he said: "Fair kinswoman! Thine upward glance stirs wonder in the breasts of ten thousand men, thy downward glance stirs joy. Yet he that names himself lord of the ten great regions of the earth hath forsaken thee, and dwells in ease by Lady Rogmo's side, leaving thee desolate. Were thy faith pledged to me, O lovely one, I would not so offend thee, but I would set thee above my lesser wives, and thou shouldst rule my household and order all things to thine own desire."

"Alas, great prince, what wickedness hast thou uttered! May the ears of all that have heard thy words be deafened, may their eyes burst from their heads! And do ye bear me witness, blue heavens, bear witness, mother earth! that if ten thousand Chotongs came to woo me, they would be to me less than the shadow of my Gessar Khan. Now come within, Prince Chotong, and eat and drink, then go thy way in peace."

And Chotong entered the yurta, and Aralgo placed savory fare before him, and he ate of the food and drank of the sweet tea, then went his way.

But after seven days he returned again to the Valley of Pleasant Winds and said to Aralgo: "Thou maiden whom men call Ten Thousand Joys, Gessar hath cast thee off. Wherefore I pray thee, lay thy hand in mine and pledge to me thy faith."

But Aralgo answered: "Lightly dost thou regard the words, Prince Chotong, that seven days since I gave thee. It cannot be that thou dost utter the will of my lord, for often have I heard him name thee a shabby fellow and of little

82

worth. Nay, thou alone hast offended against me and thou alone shalt pay the penalty."

And she lifted up her voice and cried: "Vassals and herdsmen! beat me this Chotong soundly from the Valley with staff and scourge, that nevermore may he be minded to journey hither."

And they fell upon Chotong and beat him with staff and scourge till their arms grew weary. And they took from him his russet mare, and drove him forth afoot from the Valley, and so grievous were his hurts that he came not again to Tibet before three full moons.

But when he was healed of his wounds, he bethought himself how he should wreak his vengeance upon the Lady Aralgo. And he girded his weapons about him, and laid in his scrip food for a hundred days, and took his way to the Cavern of Curses.

And there he bowed him down and cried: "Thou Spirit of the Cavern, that lends guidance to all who ask, whether for joy or sorrow, come to me in a dream, and reveal to me how I may wreak vengeance upon the Lady Aralgo, who hath wronged me."

And for thrice three and thirty days Chotong sat before the Cavern of Curses, awaiting a sign, but the Spirit of the Cavern was mute. And at length he cried: "Dost thou lack power or will, O silent Cavern, to lend me guidance? For I, Chotong, have waited thrice three and thirty days upon thy pleasure, and my scrip is empty of food and my soul of patience, and still thou hast made no sign. Wouldst thou have me perish of hunger, unfeeling spirit, before thy very portal?"

And in the night the Spirit of the Cavern appeared to Chotong in a dream, and revealed to him how he should wreak vengeance upon the Lady of Ten Thousand Joys.

And he returned to the Valley of Pleasant Winds, and in the distance the herdsmen espied him. And they gathered their flocks together, the shepherds and cowherds, the herders of steeds and of camels, and themselves they placed in their midst.

And Chotong drew nigh and cried: "How fare your flocks, good herdsmen? Do their numbers increase or abate from day to day? Do your beasts grow lean or fat?"

And their leader answered: "What is it to thee, Chotong, if our flocks increase or abate from day to day? Wilt thou reward our care if they grow fat or flog us for their leanness?"

And Chotong cried: "Death for thine insolence!" and raised his hand to smite. But the leader of the herdsmen rallied his men about him with shout and clamor, crying: "To me, ye vassals and all that serve the Lady Aralgo! Chotong is come to rob us of our herds and bear away our mistress."

And they surrounded Chotong and beat him with staff and scourge, but their blows fell harmless about him, for he was guarded by the Spirit of the Cavern whose aid he had invoked. And in the end the herdsmen released him and drove him forth again from the Valley.

But when night fell, he stole to the marshland where the swineherds tended their swine, and he questioned them, saying: "Are ye content with your lot, ye swineherds of the Lady Aralgo?"

And they answered: "Why, is there aught of pleasure in our lot that we should be content? The cowherds and the shepherds pasture their flocks in pleasant places, while they that guard the camels and the steeds may gallop at will to far-off fields and distant mountains. But we alone of all the herdsmen must abide in this foul morass, though the rains drench and the droughts parch and the winds pierce us through."

And Chotong answered: "Truly a sorry plight! And would ye be uplifted above your fellows and blessed beyond all men?"

"That would we."

"Then do but my bidding, and the cowherds and the shepherds, and they that guard the camels and the steeds, shall bow down before you, and none of all the tribe shall be exalted above the swineherds of the Lady Aralgo."

And the swineherds in their folly heeded Chotong's false words, and cried: "What is thy will? Reveal it to us, that we may do thy bidding, and be exalted above our fellows."

And Chotong revealed his will to them and departed from the Valley of Pleasant Winds.

And at midnight when the tapers were quenched, the swineherds filled three wooden troughs, according to the word of Chotong, the first with blood, the second with brandy thrice distilled, the third with sour milk. And they

86

set them down before the portal of the Lady Aralgo, and cried: "Mistress, awake! The kine suckle their young!"

And Aralgo awoke and cried: "How many kine?"

And they answered: "A hundred kine suckle their young."

And Aralgo replied: "It is well," and slept again.

But scarcely was she sunk anew in slumber than the swineherds cried: "Mistress, awake! The kine suckle their young!"

And she awoke and cried: "How many kine?"

And they answered: "A thousand kine suckle their young."

And Aralgo replied: "It is well," and slept again.

But now the swineherds clamored once more before her portal, crying: "Mistress, awake! The kine suckle their young."

And she awoke and cried: "How many kine?"

And they answered: "All the kine suckle their young."

And the Lady Aralgo leaped from her couch, crying: "My people will lack milk," and hastened without. But as she crossed the threshold of her yurta, she overturned the wooden troughs, and poured upon the earth the blood, the brandy and the sour milk, and their noxious fumes mingled together and were borne by an unfriendly wind into Tibet.

And straightway the people of Tibet were stricken with disease and pestilence, and he that was most grievously afflicted was Gessar Khan. And the Lady Rogmo betook herself to the soothsayers and cried: "Ye sages of Tibet! Our people are stricken with disease and pestilence, and Gessar Khan, our lord, droops on his couch of some strange malady. Read me your signs, therefore, ye from whom no mystery is hidden, and say whence comes this fearsome scourge upon us."

And the soothsayers took the crimson threads of prophecy and read the signs and answered: "It is a scourge borne hither from the Valley of Pleasant Winds, where dwells the Lady of Ten Thousand Joys whom Gessar took to be his second wife."

"And how shall we subdue it, that Gessar and our people may be healed of their affliction?"

"Neither Gessar nor our people will be healed till the Lady Aralgo be driven forth out of her dwelling-place, for the curse that hath been laid upon her is a bitter curse, boding disaster, and our magic hath no power to destroy it."

And the Lady Rogmo sent two couriers to the Valley of Pleasant Winds and bade them say to Gessar's second wife: "The evil that is come upon our people and Gessar Khan, our lord, proceeds from thee. Wherefore do thou depart out of this place and go whither thou wilt, that Gessar's strength may be restored to him, and the curse lifted that hath been laid upon our people."

And when the couriers had brought this word to the Lady Aralgo, she questioned them, saying: "Is it Gessar Khan, my lord, that drives me forth, or do ye bring the word of the Lady Rogmo or the vile Prince Chotong?"

And the couriers answered: "Nay, it is Gessar Khan that drives thee forth."

And the eyes of the Lady Aralgo flashed with anger, and she cried: "Ye lie, false knaves! For why should my belovèd Gessar betray me, that have kept faith with him? Nay, ye are sent by Chotong or the Lady Rogmo, and not by Gessar Khan, whose strength may the gods swiftly restore to him! Return, then, to those ye serve and say: 'The Lady Aralgo bows to your will, but the sorrows ye have sown for her today, ye shall reap yourselves tomorrow!'"

And the Lady Aralgo went forth from the Valley of Pleasant Winds alone and unbefriended, and wandered up and down the face of the earth, and knew not where she should seek shelter.

And presently she came to a strange country whose trees and streams, mountains and flowering meadows were white as ivory. And a white hare bowed down before her and said: "Thou art destined for our master," and led her to the border of his land.

And having crossed the border, she found herself within a kingdom whose trees and streams, mountains and flowering meadows were blue as turquoise. And a blue wolf bowed down before her and said: "Thou art destined for our master," and led her to the border of his land.

And having crossed the border, she came to a fair realm, whose trees and streams, mountains and flowering meadows were colored with the rainbow's changing hues. And a magpie bowed down before her and said: "Thou art destined for our master," and led her to the shore of a dark sea. And now a burning wind swept over her, scorching her with its flame, and now an icy blast descended upon her and smote her to the earth. And when she would have stood upright, she could not, so fiercely was she buffeted on either hand.

And she cried out in terror: "Protect me, gods of my father! Protect me, Gessar, whom I never wronged!" And the darkness lifted, and the winds ceased from blowing, and Aralgo beheld before her a creature whose body bore twelve heads, and on each head the upper lip ascended to the skies, while the lower lip hung downward and touched the earth. And Aralgo knew him for the twelve-headed giant, and guile entered her heart.

And she cried: "What creature art thou whose splendor dazzles my sight? Art thou Kormuzda, father of the gods? Art thou the proudest of the dragon-princes? Or can it be indeed that I have reached the goal of my wandering, and found him whom I seek?"

"Whom dost thou seek?"

"The giant with twelve heads."

"What wouldst thou of the giant with twelve heads?"

"Know, radiant being, that when Gessar Khan, lord of the ten great regions of the earth, withdrew his favor from me, I vowed to journey up and down the land till I had found the giant with twelve heads. For I would be his slave, to milk his kine or cleanse his hearth of ashes. Yea, any humble task would I perform, so I might dwell in the shadow of his glory."

And the giant bellowed with laughter that shook the mountains and troubled the waves of the sea, and when his mirth was spent, he spoke and said: "Truly, thy words sound pleasantly in mine ears as the breaking of bones, and I have no wish to harm thee. For ofttimes have I heard thy beauty praised, and ofttimes thought to take thee for my wife. Yet Gessar Khan, thy lord, is a foe not lightly to be challenged, wherefore I have left thee unmolested upon thy hillside. But now thou art come freely into my kingdom and none shall take thee from me, nay, not Gessar himself. Nor shalt thou be my slave, to milk my kine or cleanse my hearth of ashes, but my cherished wife and mistress of my household."

So saying, he seized her beneath his arm and bore her away to his castle that crowned the summit of the highest mountain. And he bade her await him in the courtyard of the castle, and himself he entered within, and as his wives came forth to greet him and bowed before him, he devoured each one in turn till none remained save only two or three. Then, summoning his vassals together, he cried: "I proclaim the Lady Aralgo my cherished wife and mistress of my household," and he led her to his throne of ebony, and seated her beside him.

Thus did the Lady of Ten Thousand Joys break faith with Gessar, plighting her troth to the twelve-headed giant.

And now the people of Tibet were freed of disease and pestilence, and Gessar Khan arose from his couch, restored to strength. And he spoke to the Lady Rogmo and said: "Beloved wife! long have I lain in suffering upon my couch, and many moons have vanished since I brought the Lady Aralgo from China and left her in the Valley of Pleasant Winds. Now I will go thither, lest she should weep for sorrow that I have forsaken her. Let my brown wonder-steed be saddled for the journey!"

And the Lady Rogmo answered: "Thy command, O destroyer of the roots of evil, is as the command of the Fearful Ones, swiftly fulfilled. Yet wherefore wilt thou saddle thy brown wonder-steed, since she whom thou wouldst comfort is departed out of the Valley of Pleasant Winds, and gone who knows whither?"

Now Gessar was sorely troubled by these tidings, and he called before him the Lord Shikeer, and the thirty heroes, and the three hundred chieftains of the tribes and his uncle Chotong. And he questioned them, saying: "Which of you can reveal to me whither the Lady Aralgo is departed from the Valley of Pleasant Winds, that I may go in quest of her?"

And the Lord Shikeer and the thirty heroes and the three hundred chieftains of the tribes were silent, but Chotong stepped forth and spoke.

"Son of the everlasting gods, Chotong will answer thee. Because she deemed herself forsaken of thy love, the Lady of Ten Thousand Joys is departed out of the Valley and dwells, men say, with the twelve-headed giant. Wherefore spend not thy strength in vain journeyings, but abide among us, and grant thyself and thy steed the blessing of sweet repose."

"Sage counsel from a fool, uncle Chotong! If my wife is gone freely to the twelve-headed giant, I will seek her out and slay her, that her sin against me may be atoned. But

93

if the giant have taken her perforce, then will I slay the giant and take my wife back to the Valley of Pleasant Winds."

But when the lamas and the holy men learned of their master's purpose, they counselled him against it, crying: "Forsake us not, thou that hast brought light out of darkness, for the stars frown upon this enterprise."

But Gessar answered: "Wise lamas consider how they may redeem the souls of men, and foolish ones how they may fill their bellies without toil. But when ye would give counsel to Gessar Khan, ye are as two calves bound to a tree, beating your heads against your fellow's flank. Observe your vows and fast, ye pious ones, and go your ways."

And now the ministers approached and bowed before him and cried: "Forsake us not, O thou that hast wrought peace out of confusion!"

But Gessar answered: "Do ye administer while I am gone the law I have given you, and judge not by the semblance of the man, but read his heart."

Then the three hundred chieftains of the tribes abased themselves before him and cried: "Forsake us not, belovèd of the gods, whose breast is as a bulwark before the foe."

But Gessar answered: "It may be that the foe prepares even now to march against you and give you battle. Return then to your tents, and look to your armor and your helmets, lest they lose their lustre, and to your weapons, lest their edge be dulled."

And the lamas and the ministers and the three hundred chieftains of the tribes departed from the presence of Gessar Khan.

And Gessar donned his armor that sparkled like the dew at dawn, and his helmet wrought of the light of the sun and moon. And he girded about him his lightning sword three fathoms long, and his ebon bow, and his thirty silver arrows notched with turquoise. And his brown wonder-steed, arrayed in the skin of a tiger, was led before him, and he mounted upon his back.

And the Lady Rogmo brought food for Gessar, lest he hunger upon the way, and about the neck of his steed she laid garlands of sugar and of raisins. And she exhorted them, crying: "Brown wonder-steed! Shouldst thou lack heart or strength to bring my lord to the end of his journeying, I will shear thee of mane and tail, and burn thy body to ashes. Gessar, my noble lord, shouldst thou lag behind thy steed in cunning or prowess, thy thumbs shall be slit like a craven's and cast to the flames, and nevermore will I look upon thy face."

And Gessar answered: "Thy words are eagles' wings to uplift my spirit," and taking leave of the Lady Rogmo, he set forth upon his journey.

But ever and again as he rode, he turned his head to gaze upon her where she stood in the shadow of her yurta, until at length his steed rebuked him and cried: "Why dost thou twist thy head like a calf in search of his mother? Thy road lies onward, not back. If thy heart be in this task, let thine eyes follow. If not, return as thou camest."

And Gessar said: "Thou dost well to upbraid me, my brown one," and he fixed his eyes before him, and journeyed onward toward the realm of the twelve-headed giant.

And Cæsar donned his armor that sparkled like the dew at dawn, and his helmet wrought of the light of the sun and moon. And he girded about him his lightning sword three fathoms long, and his ebon bow and his thirty silver arrows notched with turquoise. And his brown wonder-steed, arrayed in the skin of a tiger, was led before him, and he mounted upon his back.

And the Lady Rogmo brought food for Cæsar, lest he hunger upon the way, and about the neck of his steed she laid garlands of sugar and of raisins. And she exhorted them, crying,

But ever and again as he rode, he turned his head to gaze upon her where she stood, in the shadow of her yurta, until at length his steed rebuked him and cried, "Why dost thou twist thy head like a calf in search of his mother? Thy road lies onward, not back. If thy heart be in this task, let thine eyes follow. If not, return as thou camest."

And Cæsar said, "Thou dost well to upbraid me, my brown one," and he fixed his eyes before him, and journeyed onward toward the realm of the twelve-headed giant.

V. THE TWELVE-HEADED GIANT

O F THE PERILS ENCOUNTERED BY GESSAR IN
HIS JOURNEY AGAINST THE TWELVE-
HEADED GIANT, AND HOW HE SLEW HIM AT
LAST, AND DRANK THE DRINK OF FORGETFULNESS.

Now as Gessar journeyed toward the realm of the twelve-
headed giant, he came to the foot of a high mountain. And
leaving his steed to gambol in the valley below, he scaled
the mountain to its very peak, and stood upon the summit
and cried: "Ye, my three sisters! I go to do battle with the
giant that hath stolen away the Lady Aralgo. Hearten me

with your counsel! Inform me with your wisdom! It is I, your brother, that calls!"

And his three sisters appeared to him in the guise of a cuckoo and said: "Beloved brother! Thy task is no simple one, yet guided by our wisdom, it may be thou wilt gain the victory over thy foe. Hear now our counsel. Presently thou shalt enter into a forest where roams a bull so huge that he devours three pastures at a gulp, and drains the waters of three rivers from source to mouth. Him must thou slay ere thou canst enter into the realm of the twelve-headed giant. Go warily, lest he overpower thee, yet boldly, lest he mock thee for a coward. And from Sumeru our love shall shelter thee." So saying, the cuckoo spread her wings and soared aloft.

And Gessar went down from the mountain and journeyed farther. But darkness descended upon the land, and he could see neither to right nor to left, nor above nor before him, neither the palm of his hand nor the ears of his wonder-steed. Wherefore he dismounted, and made of his cloak a pillow for his head, and turned his countenance toward the eastern sky, and laid himself to rest upon the earth.

And as he slept, the Wild Bull of the Forest stole softly on Gessar's wonder-steed, and thrusting forth his tongue, stripped him at once of mane and tail; and thrusting forth his tongue a second time, stripped Gessar's silver arrows of their plumage.

And the steed cried: "Thou churlish bull! Gessar shall know of the affront thou hast put upon him!"

And the bull taunted him, crying: "On the morrow will

I swallow thee and Gessar, as now I have swallowed thy goodly mane and tail," and so departed.

And Gessar awoke at dawn, and saw that his steed had been stripped of mane and tail, and stood abashed before him, and that his arrows, like the arrows of a babe, were bare of plumage. And he made plaint and cried: "Ye dwellers in the sky, is this the shelter and the care ye pledged me? Lo, as ye slumbered all on Sumeru, the Wild Bull of the Forest thrust forth his tongue, stripping my wonder-steed of mane and tail, and my thirty silver arrows of their plumage!"

And his three sisters appeared to him in the guise of a cuckoo and cried: "Art thou a woman, brother, that thou dost rend the earth and sky with thy clamor? If thou wouldst weep, abandon this enterprise and return to the shelter of thy yurta. But if thou wouldst journey farther and reach thy goal, spend not thy strength in childish lamentation. The bank that resists the onslaught of the waves shall be the staunchest boulder, and he that falters not in the face of disaster, his valor shall be as the finest flint, for none shall destroy it. Wherefore lay our words to thy heart, dear brother, and weep no longer. We will restore the plumage of thine arrows, and thou shalt judge whether their lustre be dimmed or brightened. And for thy steed, let him feed thrice ere midday on the wheat that covers yonder field, and his mane and tail shall flourish again in splendor on his back."

And they restored the plumage of Gessar's arrows, and Gessar looked on them where they lay in his quiver, and saw that their lustre was brighter than of yore. And thrice ere midday he led his wonder-steed to the field of wheat and bade him eat thereof, and when he had eaten thrice, his mane and tail flourished again in splendor on his back. And Gessar bestrode him and said: "Do thou follow the footprints of the Bull as he roams through the forest, and overtake him, else will I slash thy four hoofs from thy legs and strip thee of saddle and bridle, and journey homeward afoot."

And the steed answered: "Doubt me not, master, I will do my part, but look to thine own labor. For thou must send thine arrow through the mark upon the Wild Bull's brow, and should it swerve by so much as the breadth of a hair, I will fling thee from my back and return to thy glorious sisters on Sumeru."

And Gessar cried: "Well spoken!" and smote his wonder-steed so sharp a blow that he soared aloft and galloped through the air. And Gessar sought to restrain him, crying: "Art thou become a falcon or a hawk that suddenly thou art minded to ply the heavens? I prithee, go softly on the surface of the earth, dear comrade, as thou art wont, and if in my haste I smote thee too sharp a blow, humbly I seek thy pardon."

And the brown wonder-steed descended to the surface of the earth, and followed the Wild Bull's footprints, and presently they came upon him where he felled with his horn's tip three oaks that barred his way to a pleasant stream.

And the steed cried out: "Ho, thou Wild Bull! Gessar is come, whose steed thou didst despoil of mane and tail, and his arrows of their plumage."

And the Wild Bull answered: "I welcome him, for now I will devour arrows and steed and Gessar Khan himself."

So saying, he leaped upon them, but Gessar's arrow found him in midair, and pierced the snowy ring that marked his brow, and laid him low. And the earth shuddered and the forest groaned beneath his fall.

And Gessar, rejoicing, plunged his sword into the Wild Bull's throat, and carved a tender morsel, that he might partake of the flesh of his enemy, but when he would have thrust it into his mouth, his sisters appeared to him in their proper guise and cried: "Stay, Gessar! As a hero hast thou assailed thy foe and as a master slain him! But as a glutton dost thou fall upon him now to gorge thee with his flesh. Yea, eat thy fill, good brother, but not till thou hast offered sacrifice to all the gods in turn, and to thy sisters who have watched above thee from Sumeru."

And Gessar repented him of his folly and cried: "In truth, I know not why I fell thus rashly upon him, whether to sate my hunger or my rage. Forgive me my sin, ye heavenly ones, and take at my hands this offering that I make you of the unsullied flesh of the Wild Bull."

And he built a fire and scattered incense upon it, and offered up a sacrifice to the gods of the Wild Bull's flesh. And when they had accepted the sacrifice, he and his steed feasted on what remained.

And now his sisters said: "Thou must proceed alone, beloved Gessar, for the way is foul with all manner of abominations, and we may not venture farther. Thou wilt come soon to an enchanted river, upon whose waters headless men and trunkless horses float hither and yon. And they will rend the air with shrieks and moans and horrid clamor, seeking to affright thee, yet do thou pay no heed, but smite the waters thrice with thy magic sword and cross in safety to the farther shore. Continue onward, and ere long thou wilt see before thee two walls of rock, standing so close one to the other that a shadow may not pass between them. But how thou shalt overcome this barrier and many besides that the giant will prepare for thee, thou must ask of thy dauntless heart and thy nimble wit!" And the sisters vanished.

And Gessar journeyed onward till he came to the enchanted river, upon whose waters headless men and trunkless horses floated hither and yon. And they rent the air with shrieks and moans and horrid clamor, seeking to affright him, yet he paid no heed, but smote the waters thrice with his magic sword and crossed in safety to the farther shore.

And he rode onward till he saw before him two walls of rock, standing so close one to the other that a shadow might not pass between them. And he cried aloud: "In Tibet I have seen two walls of rock part from each other, disclosing a passage for man and steed. Yet when man and steed have arrived within their shadow, they have come together, crushing the travelers in their cruel embrace. But these rocks that guard the realm of the twelve-headed giant are witless rocks, unknowing of their power."

And the rocks heard the words of Gessar and said one to the other: "Shall we suffer the rocks of Tibet to outdo us in guile? Let us go asunder, and when this horseman rides within our shadow, let us come together and destroy him, that never again may he extol the power of other rocks above our power."

And they went asunder, disclosing a passage for man and steed. But Gessar sped so swiftly through the gap that ere they could come together to destroy him, he had emerged in safety beyond their reach. And they were angered that he had escaped them, and crashed so fiercely upon one another that they were shattered, and fell in many fragments to the earth.

And he journeyed onward, and came at length upon a herdsman who tended camels. And he cried: "Herdsman, where lies the castle of the giant?"

"Yonder it lies upon the summit of the highest mountain."

"Is the way smooth or rugged that I must follow, and what monsters lie in my path?"

"The way is rugged, and the ridges are kept by watchful sentinels—the pearly ridge by the sons of the shining gods, the golden ridge by the sons of mortal men, the ebon ridge by the sons of the giants themselves. Thou must answer to all three ere they will suffer thee to seek the giant's castle."

And Gessar gave thanks to the herdsman and journeyed onward until he came to the pearly ridge that was guarded by the sons of the shining gods. And when they saw him, they lifted up their voices and cried: "Alas, red-footed mortal! Our master will slay us, should he learn of thy presence here! Go swiftly hence again!"

"And if I will not?"

"Then art thou no mortal, but one mightier than he.

Can it be indeed that thou art Gessar Khan, lord of the ten great regions of the earth, whose coming hath been foretold to us? How may we know thee?"

"I am he indeed, lord of the ten great regions of the earth, whose coming hath been foretold to you. Fear me not, but draw nigh, ye children of the gods, and reveal to me wherefore ye serve the giant, since his ways are evil ways!"

"Unmindful of our parents' bidding, we left the heavens to frolic for an hour in the fields of men. But ere we had alighted upon the earth, the giant seized us and bore us hither, to guard this pearly ridge against his foe."

"Then how will ye reward me if I slay this giant and free you from his power?"

"Nay, if thou go to slay him, we will give thee counsel to guide thee, and treasures to ease thy toil. The golden ridge above us is guarded by the children of men. They too are unwilling sentinels, and when thou hast revealed thyself to them, they will speed thee on thy way. But the ebon ridge is guarded by the children of the giants who are thine enemy. How thou shalt overcome them we know not, but when this task is done, enter the forest that will loom before thee, and journey through it, paying no heed to aught thou shalt see or hear. Thou wilt issue forth at the foot of a lofty peak upon whose summit lies the giant's castle. But this peak is shrouded in mists so dense that day and night are one, and neither man nor beast may find the path wherein to set his foot. Take then this golden and this silver net, and when the mists engulf thee, cast them into the skies, and they will snare the sun and moon to light thy darkness."

And Gessar took the nets, and journeyed to the golden

ridge that was guarded by the sons of men. And they rejoiced that he was come to deliver them from bondage, and sped him on his way.

And now he came to the ebon ridge that was guarded by the sons of the giants. And dismounting, he offered up a baling to the gods in sacrifice, and besought them, crying: "Ye blessèd ones, whose power is unending! Unloose your dragons' thunder! Let fly your lightning shafts! And amid the uproar send a shower of hailstones, huge as my doubled fist, to crush the heads of these sentinels, for your Gessar would ascend the perilous peak to do battle with his enemy!"

And the gods heeded his prayers, and let fly their lightning shafts, and yoked their dragons to the chariots, and their voices thundered to one another across the skies. And when the uproar reached the ears of the giants, they were dismayed and flung themselves to the earth, but a shower of hailstones huge as the doubled fist of Gessar descended upon them, crushing their heads. And Gessar passed between them.

And journeying farther, he entered a dark forest where shimnus in the guise of beauteous maidens beckoned to him and sweet voices called, but he paid no heed to aught that he saw or heard, and issued forth at the foot of a lofty peak, shrouded in mists so dense that day and night were one and he knew not whither to guide his wonder-steed. And he cast his nets into the sky, and in his golden net he snared the sun, and the moon in his silver net, and by their light he ascended the perilous peak and reached its summit.

And he saw before him the walls of the giant's castle, but

he could find no portal to give him entrance, and he said to his wonder-steed: "Bear me aloft as thou didst bear me in the wilderness, then plunging downward like a golden arrow, set me within the walls of the giant's castle. Beware, for if thou fail me in this, I will slash thy hoofs from thy legs and journey homeward afoot. But if I fail and fall from thy back and perish, may my unworthy flesh be devoured by hounds!"

"Alack, dear master, when have I begrudged thee my magic power, that thou shouldst barter thus with if and if! Withdraw but to a distance of thirty paces from the castle walls and, urging me forward with voice and hand, cry: 'On! On, thou flower of Kormuzda's herd!' and thou shalt see how bravely I will serve thee."

And Gessar withdrew to a distance of thirty paces from the castle walls, and seizing the reins in his left hand, and pressing hard his legs against the flanks of his wonder-steed, with his right hand he smote him thrice and cried: "On! On, thou flower of Kormuzda's herd!" And the steed galloped to the castle walls, then soared aloft and, plunging downward like a golden arrow, set Gessar Khan within.

And Gessar cried: "Thou hast served me bravely, my faithful one, and now thou shalt take thine ease. Return to Sumeru, and bed thyself in Kormuzda's heavenly stalls, and feed on heavenly fodder, and slake thy thirst in the waters of heavenly streams. And when I have need of thee again, I will summon thee."

And the wonder-steed gave thanks to his master, and lifted up his voice and cried: "Thou Keeper of Kormuzda's blessèd steeds! Let down a ladder that I may ascend to thee!"

"Who would ascend?"

"I, the brown wonder-steed!"

And the Keeper of Kormuzda's steeds let down a hempen ladder, binding one end to Sumeru's silver peak, while the other end swung free above the earth.

But the brown wonder-steed, at sight of the hempen ladder, roared in anger, and his nostrils belched black smoke and his eyes spat flame, and he cried: "How should this hempen ladder bear my weight? Am I a foal or Gessar's brown wonder-steed? Ere I were come halfway, it would break asunder and send me crashing to earth. Draw it back, thou heedless Keeper, and let down another ladder of strong chains!"

And the Keeper of the steeds drew back the hempen ladder and let down a ladder of strong chains whereon the brown wonder-steed ascended to Sumeru.

And when he was departed, Gessar approached the castle that rose before him, its silver roof crowned by a chimney of rubies. And he cried: "Where bides the lord and where the lady of this silver castle?"

And Aralgo heard his voice from within and flung the portal wide. And weeping, she cast herself into his arms and cried: "As the golden sun dost thou rise upon my darkness, O heaven-born!"

And Gessar chided her, saying: "Art thou not in sooth a woman of little wit, weeping when thou shouldst laugh? Nay, dry thy tears and say why thou didst leave the Valley of Pleasant Winds to journey hither. For if the giant took thee perforce, I will slay him, but if thou didst go freely I must needs slay thee, that thy sin against me may be atoned."

And Aralgo told him all as it befell, and Gessar cried: "Thou hast been ill-used, and Chotong shall answer to me for his deed. But now I would seek out the giant and challenge him, and may the victory be his whom the gods love."

"Yet how if he should slay thee, my Gessar? For this is a monster so fearful as in all thine exploits thou hast not encountered. Nay, thou wert best flee for thy life, ere he return from the chase to find thee here."

"Dost thou give this counsel to some untried stripling, or to the chosen son of the gods? Enough of parley, and say whither I may go in search of him."

"If thou be resolved to challenge him, tarry a little till I have beguiled him of his secrets. When the sun is red, he will return from the chase, riding his mule of copper-green, and bearing a hornèd moose upon his back, and when he hath eaten and drunk to his content, I will question him, and from a hidden place thou shalt hear his words."

And they entered the castle and came to a marble chamber, in whose floor a jewel burned. And Aralgo touched the jewel and it vanished, disclosing a deep pit. But when Gessar had crept within the pit, the jewel appeared again, and all was as it had been.

And when the sun was red, the giant returned, riding his mule of copper-green, and bearing a hornèd moose upon his back. And he roared: "Let my small pike be brought, that I may dislodge the crumbs of my morning meal!"

And his small pike was brought, and from the crevices of his teeth he dislodged the bones of forty men and let them fall to earth. Then, entering his marble chamber, he sat him down to a feast of roasted elephants and lions.

And when he had eaten and drunk to his content, he summoned the Lady of Ten Thousand Joys to bear him company. And she sat at his feet and laid her white hand in his and, gazing upon him, said: "My matchless husband, dearer than all the world to my heart, I am oppressed with fear lest one day the odious Gessar should come and challenge thee to combat."

"Fear not, my tender one, for with my weakest finger I will crush him and fling him back again into Tibet."

"Nay, he is not so lightly crushed nor flung into Tibet. Wherefore, I pray thee, tell me how thou wilt defend thyself against him, that I may be unburdened of my sorrow."

"Naught will I tell thee, for he that hath learned wisdom counts no bush a tree, nor no hawk a bird, nor no woman his friend."

"What empty speech is this! Yea, now I do bethink me how when I came thy beauteous wives all vanished down thy gullet, that I might reign supreme. Dost thou think now to condemn me to their horrid fate, having found another fairer than Aralgo? Woe, woe is me! Would that the noble Gessar might come and slay me, wretched that I am!" And Aralgo cast herself upon the ground, uttering grievous cries and lamentations.

And the giant said: "Cease thy lamentations and draw nigh again, for I have found none fairer than thee."

But Aralgo would not, and at length he cried: "I will reveal to thee all my mysteries if thou wilt but raise thy head from the ground and smile upon me."

And Aralgo raised her head from the ground and smiled upon him, and the giant said: "Gessar may not slay me till he have slain my younger sister, who inhabits the topmost branches of the Tree of Delight in the kingdom to the east. Nor may he slay me till he have slain my elder sister, who is a mighty yaksha, and dwells in the kingdom to the west. But first he must gain possession of the beetle that she hath hidden away and destroy it, for the beetle is thy husband's soul that his sister jealously guards. Should Gessar succeed in all these undertakings, still he must put to death the golden fish that slips from my right nostril as I sleep and plays on my right shoulder; and the silver fish that slips from my left nostril as I sleep and plays on my left shoulder. These deeds being done, he will not overthrow me till he have severed from my shoulders my twelve heads. Judge then, my Lady of Ten Thousand Joys, if I be not well defended from this Gessar."

"Thou art a creature whose like walks not upon the earth, nor soars through the blue heavens nor peoples the sea. And that thou art my husband and I thy wife, I count as a great blessing."

And the giant rejoiced in Aralgo's words of praise, and laid him down to sleep. And when the day broke, he arose again and, mounting his copper-green mule, went forth to the chase.

And Aralgo touched the jewel that burned in the floor

and it vanished, but when Gessar had emerged out of the pit, the jewel appeared again and all was as it had been. And he strode forth from the castle, and in the court he lifted up his voice and cried: "Brown wonder-steed! Gessar hath. need of thee!"

And from the heavens the ladder of strong chains was let down and the brown wonder-steed descended. And his comrades flung ashes after him, crying: "Farewell, brown wonder-steed!" as was their wont when one departed from their midst. And the ashes were transformed into cloudlets that sailed in the sky.

But the brown wonder-steed bore Gessar over the castle walls and into the kingdom on the east, where he found the Tree of Delight in whose topmost branches the giant's younger sister dwelt.

And he stood at its foot and spoke aloud and said: "Surely this is a daughter of the gods, or of the dragon-princes, or it may be of Gessar Khan himself, for in all my journeying I have not beheld a maid so wondrous fair. Would she might descend from the branches to hold speech with me! Yet can it be that mine eyes have played me false, and that this creature is no maid indeed, but a magpie or a crow? For why should a beauteous damsel spend her days in the branches of a tree?"

And the maiden thought: "Truly this youth speaks with the wisdom of age. Am I a bird that I should inhabit the branches of a tree? I will go down to him."

And she descended, and stood at Gessar's side, and said to him: "Who and whence art thou?"

"I come from the Everlasting Realm, whose black-capped lama gave me ere I left a necklet of many strands to be my talisman. Shall I give it to thee?"

"Why not? Fain would I wear the talisman of the black-capped lama."

"Wilt thou wear it about thine ankles or thy tender throat?"

"Wherefore about mine ankles? Nay, I will wear it on my tender throat as necklets should be worn."

"Suffer me then, in exchange for my talisman, to lay it there," and Gessar took from his bosom three bowstrings, and laid them about the throat of the giant's sister and drew them fast, till the breath left her body and she fell at the foot of the tree. And the skin of her tender throat was transformed to scales, and her body to the body of a reptile. And kindling a blaze that consumed reptile and tree, Gessar turned back again to the giant's castle.

And when the sun was red the giant, mounted upon his mule of copper-green, returned from the chase. And he said to Aralgo: "Alack! Four of my heads throb with such grievous pangs as they had been cleft by bludgeons."

And Aralgo answered: "Belike thou didst capture naught for thy midday meal, and thy pangs are the pangs of hunger."

"Nay, for I captured three herds of yak, together with their herdsman, and feasted abundantly."

"Then go not forth, I pray thee, on the morrow, but bide at home that I may minister unto thee."

"Am I a babe that I should bide at home for an aching

head?" And on the morrow the giant bound up four of his heads in snowy kerchiefs and went forth to the chase.

And when he was departed, Gessar summoned his wonder-steed from Sumeru, and journeyed to the kingdom on the west. And there a yellow hind leaped before him and, taking aim, he let fly his arrow from the bow, and the arrow pierced the brow of the hind and thrust its head forth from her shining flank.

And the hind was transformed into a yaksha, whose upper lip ascended to the skies, while her lower lip hung downward and touched the earth. And she seized the arrow's plumage at her brow, seeking to draw the dart from the wound, but she could not; and she seized the arrow's head at her side, seeking to dislodge it, but in vain.

And she cried: "Who art thou, youth?"

And he answered: "Dost thou not know me, yaksha?"

"Nay, for till this hour, may it be accurst, I have never beheld thee."

"Am I not the giant and thy younger brother?"

"The giant and my brother! If this be truth, thou art grown passing fair. When didst thou put off thy wonted guise, and assume the body of a comely youth?"

"When I took the Lady Aralgo to wife."

"And wherefore didst thou wound me even now with an arrow from thy bow?"

"Out of the hatred that I bear thee, for since my birth thou hast jealously guarded the beetle that is my soul, nor vouchsafed me a glimpse of it."

"Because I knew thy rashness and feared lest thou

117

shouldst imperil thy soul, therefore I kept it from thee."

"Let me look upon it now, and when I have looked my fill, I will draw the arrow out of thy wound."

And the yaksha hurled the beetle at Gessar's feet and he trod upon it. Then seizing the arrow's plumage at her brow, he drew the dart from the wound, but plunged it again into her evil heart and she fell lifeless before him. And kindling a blaze that consumed yaksha and beetle, Gessar turned back again to the giant's castle.

And when the sun was red the giant, mounted upon his mule of copper-green, returned from the chase. And he said to Aralgo: "Eight of my heads throb in such bitter anguish as they had been riven by swords," and flinging himself upon the marble floor, he writhed in pain; but after a time he slumbered.

And a fish of gold slipped from his right nostril as he slept and played on his right shoulder; and from his left nostril slipped a silver fish and played on his left shoulder. And Gessar issued forth from his hiding place, a bludgeon in either hand, and lifting the bludgeons high above his head, he brought them down again on the giant's shoulders, slaying the golden and the silver fish and rousing his foe from slumber.

And when the giant beheld him, he bellowed in rage and sprang upon him, as a tiger springs from the crest of a mountain upon a goat. But Gessar drew forth his lightning-sword from its sheath, and ere the giant could wreak his anger upon him, he had sundered eleven heads from the monster's shoulders. And now he raised his sword to smite the last, but the giant stayed him, crying: "Thou radiant one that hast shorn me of mine honor and my heads, hold thine avenging hand! For I never injured thee, save that I took thy wife to be my wife when thou hadst abandoned her. And now I own thee my master, and with all my guile will I serve thee, and with all my magic lore uphold thy power, and together we will do battle against thy foes and destroy them utterly. And in summer we will dwell in my domain, for summer abates her ardor on this peak; but in winter we will journey to Tibet, for winter visits thee gently."

And the giant's words were pleasant in Gessar's ears, and he stayed his hand, but clear as a silver trumpet the voice of his sisters sounded from Sumeru: "False are his words as his heart is black! Slay him while yet thou canst, for the flesh of his body is turning into bronze, and soon thou shalt strike in vain!"

And straightway Gessar smote the giant's neck, but his neck was transformed to bronze, and the edge of the lightning-sword would not enter in. And he sought to thrust its point through the giant's breast, but his breast was transformed to bronze, and the point of the lightning-sword would not enter in. And swiftly he plunged his sword through the giant's paunch, and sought and pierced his heart, and when he drew his weapon forth again, he saw how the molten bronze dripped from its blade.

And now he severed the twelfth head from the giant's shoulders, and kindled a blaze that consumed him where he lay, and Aralgo cried: "Thou lion-souled! staunch as the four cliffs of Sumeru! thou hast destroyed the giant and all his kin! Drink now this cooling draught, for it is a balm against thy weariness!"

And she gave him a black draught in a golden chalice, that was the draught of forgetfulness. And he took it and drank deeply thereof, and when he had drunk, all that was befallen him since his birth fled from his memory.

VI. THE THREE SHIRAIGOL KHANS

O F THE MARCH OF THE THREE SHIRAIGOL
KHANS UPON TIBET TO SEIZE THE LADY
ROGMO, AND OF THE GLORIOUS VICTORY
WON OVER THEM BY GESSAR'S FAITHFUL HEROES.

Now it chanced on that very day when the son of heaven
and scourge of evil on earth, the all-conquering Gessar
Khan, had taken the draught of forgetfulness at the hands
of the Lady Aralgo and drunk thereof, that the three Shiraigol Khans met in council to advise with one another as to
where might be found a fair and seemly bride for the Prince

Gereltu, son of Tsagan Khan, chief of the three Khans of Shiraigol.

And Sheera Khan, the second brother, said: "Let us send couriers to the great ones of the earth, and let the couriers bring us tidings of the beauty and seemliness of their daughters."

And Chara Khan, the youngest brother, replied thereto: "And let our couriers be the birds of the air and the beasts of the wilderness that journey more swiftly over the earth than men on steeds."

And Tsagan Khan gave ear to his brothers' words, and he sent a hawk to the kingdom of Balpó, to learn if the daughter of Balpó's Khan were fair. And he sent a fox to the realm of Enedkek, to learn if the daughter of Enedkek's Khan were fair. And to the land of Tibet he sent a raven, to learn if the daughter of Gessar Khan were fair.

And after a year the hawk returned from Balpó and bowed before his masters and said: "The daughter of Balpó's Khan is fair as a new-born doe at her mother's side. Yet she is unversed in the ways of men and courts, and therefore unworthy to be our prince's bride."

And after two years the fox returned from Enedkek and bowed before his masters and said: "The daughter of Enedkek's Khan is fair as a quiet lake among sunny hills. Yet she cleaves to her father's house and is loth to leave it, and therefore she may not be Gereltu's bride."

And after three years the raven returned from Tibet and bowed before his masters, and they saw that the light of his eyes was quenched in darkness.

And Tsagan cried: "What enemy hath darkened thy sight, O raven, and what tidings dost thou bring of the daughter of Gessar Khan?"

"I bring no tidings of the daughter of Gessar Khan, for when I beheld the Lady Rogmo, his chosen wife, I quenched the light of mine eyes that they might not gaze upon glory less than hers. When she stands upright, she is like a mountain pine decked in gleaming silks. When she sits, she is like the yurta of a prince in a green valley. By sunlight she melts to a flame, by moonlight she freezes to crystal, and when she raises her head, it is as though she led ten thousand warriors to battle, so measureless is her splendor."

And Tsagan Khan said to his brothers: "If the raven speaks truly, here is a princess worthy to be the bride of Gereltu. If falsely, he is the very lord of liars. Are thy words true or false, O golden tongue?"

"True, gracious Khan! Moreover, if ye be minded to seize the Lady Rogmo, delay no longer! For Gessar tarries still in the country of the twelve-headed giant, and while he bides from home, it may be ye will thrive in your venture. But should he return again, he will surely slay you."

And the three Khans took counsel with one another, and resolved that they would journey to Tibet, that their own eyes might behold the Lady Rogmo. And they transformed themselves into a vulture so huge that his outspread wings darkened the light of the sun. And the vulture's snowy head was Tsagan Khan, and the vulture's yellow body was Sheera Khan, and the vulture's ebon tail was Chara Khan.

And so he flew to Tibet and alighted at dawn on the Lady Rogmo's yurta, causing its walls to tremble and its golden columns to sway from side to side. And Rogmo sprang from her couch and summoned the Tiger-hero, whom Gessar had named defender of his household when he rode away to do battle with the giant.

And Rogmo cried: "Brave Tiger-hero! Some monster hath alighted upon my yurta, and whether he be the giant who, having slain the son of heaven, comes now to seize his wife, I know not. Wherefore do thou stretch thy bowstring taut and lay thine arrows ready to thy hand, and we will go forth together and destroy him."

And the Tiger-hero stretched his bowstring taut and laid his arrows ready to his hand, and by the Lady Rogmo's side he went forth out of the yurta. But when he beheld the vulture, whose outspread wings darkened the light of the sun, his heart grew faint within him, and he let fall his weapons to the earth.

And Rogmo cried in scorn: "Thou Tiger-hero whose valor forsakes thee before the gaze of a bird, give me thy bow and arrows, and I will do what thy woman's heart denies thee strength to do!"

But the Tiger-hero answered: "Thou dost well to censure me, my Lady Rogmo, yet I will not yield thee my arrows and my bow, lest my shame be doubled in the eyes of my honored lord who gave thee to my care."

"Then steel thy hand to the task that lies before thee and pierce the vulture's breast!"

And the Tiger-hero laid his arrow against the bowstring,

aiming it at the vulture's breast, but his hand trembled, and the arrow swerved, striking the outspread pinion of the vulture, whose yellow feathers rained about their heads. And the bird soared aloft and, circling thrice above the Lady Rogmo, vanished from sight.

And he returned to his kingdom and, alighting upon the earth, his snowy head was transformed into Tsagan Khan, and his ebon tail was transformed into Chara Khan, and his yellow body was transformed into Sheera Khan, with a wound in his right arm.

And Tsagan said to his brothers: "What need for speech? We have seen that the raven spoke truly of Rogmo's beauty. Wherefore let us assemble our armies and march upon the hosts of Tibet, that we may seize the Lady Rogmo and bear her hither to be the bride of Gereltu, my son."

And Sheera Khan made answer: "Bethink thee well, good brother! For it is told that the mighty Gessar is a god indeed, sheathing his godhood in a mortal skin, and that his thirty heroes are such warriors as we may not hope to outdo."

And Chara Khan, the youngest brother, cried: "To capture the chosen wife of Kormuzda's son, this were a deed for the gods to frown upon. Wherefore let us abandon this undertaking, and from among the daughters of neighboring princes let us make choice of a bride for Gereltu."

"There is none among them to equal the Lady Rogmo!"

"If there be none to equal the Lady Rogmo, let us make choice of the fairest among them, and adorn her in robes as rich and jewels as bright, and name her the Lady Rogmo. Then who will be bold enough to stand forth and say: 'Thou art not the Lady Rogmo'?"

"Nay, brothers, I like not your counsel. And if it please you, ye may bide at home like men whose eyes have been shattered or whose ears have been deafened or whose bodies have been stricken by some loathsome pestilence. But for your warriors, they shall ride with me into Tibet!"

And Chara Khan answered: "Thy words are such words as are flung at cowards, O Khan, but we are accounted heroes and thy peers! Wherefore, since thou art resolved, let mead be brought, that we may pledge ourselves to this venture!"

And a golden bowl was brought, filled with strong mead, and the Khans of Shiraigol drank, and pledged themselves to march into Tibet and seize the Lady Rogmo and give her for a bride to Gereltu. And on the morrow they led forth their hosts, whose numbers were three million and three hundred thousand.

Now in Tibet the Lady Rogmo commanded that the yellow plumage shot from the vulture's wing be laden upon thirty asses, and bearing a single feather in her hand, she rode at their head to the yurta of Shikeer that lay a day and a night from Gessar's yurta.

And at dawn she came to the Stream of the Elephant, where Shikeer watered his steeds. And when he beheld her, he cried: "Why dost thou come with the dawn, fair Lady Rogmo? And is it a golden tree thou dost bear in thy hand or a feather of yellow?"

"How should I bear a tree in my hand, Shikeer? It is a feather of yellow, shot from the plumage of a mighty vulture that lighted on my tent. So huge was he that though the Tiger-hero grazed but his pinion, these thirty asses can scarce bear the weight of the plumage he dislodged."

"Was the head white?"

"White as the snow that crowns our highest mountain."

"Was the body yellow?"

"Yellow as the feathers wherewith these beasts are laden."

"Was the tail black?"

"Black as the magic coal without rift or seam."

"I know this vulture. In magic guise the Shiraigol Khans have looked on thy beauty, whereof the raven that fluttered above thee for many days gave them tidings. Would I had slain him, as I thought to do, ere weightier matters drove him from my mind. Yet there is naught to fear, for though Gessar be absent, what can these three Khans do against the comrade of his heart, Shikeer, and the thirty heroes and the three hundred chieftains of the tribes! Be of good cheer, fair Rogmo, and bide thou here till I have assembled our princes in council together."

And Shikeer assembled the princes, and all that was befallen the Lady Rogmo he recounted to them. And Chotong stepped forth and said: "The Shiraigol Khans, who have ever been our friends, are now our foes for the sake of the Lady Rogmo. Wherefore let Rogmo flee to some lonely isle in the Chatun Stream, and when the Khans learn that she is gone from our midst, they will leave us unmolested."

And Shikeer made answer: "Chotong, the soul of a flea

inhabits thy body, that looks wisely upon the world in days of peace, but utters folly when peril is at hand. Return thou to the shelter of thine abode, for we have no need of thee. But for you, ye thirty heroes and ye three hundred chieftains of the tribes, assemble your warriors! Let the battle hosts of Tangut and Tibet, on horse and foot, gather together, and let their meeting-place be the mouth of the Satsargana Stream!"

And the couriers rode forth, bearing the word of Shikeer throughout the land, and the battle hosts of Tangut and Tibet gathered together and met at the mouth of the Satsargana Stream. And they were arrayed, according to their rank, on horse and foot, and their standards were borne before them, and their chieftains rode at their head, and the thirty heroes on their fiery steeds, clad in the shining panoply of war, ranged themselves side by side, awaiting the coming of the Lord Shikeer.

And he came on his wingèd charger and, drawing rein before them, he cried: "Are the hosts assembled?"

And Shumar the Eagle-hero answered: "They are assembled."

And Shikeer cried: "Do thou, Shumar the Eagle, ride on my left! And thou, Nantsong, youngest of Gessar's heroes, on my right! Now let the trumpets sound nine blasts to herald our coming, and so we will go forth to do battle for our belovèd lord and against his foes!"

And the trumpets sounded nine blasts, and the Lord Shikeer, with Nantsong on his right, and Shumar the Eagle-hero, on his left, and all his shining warriors at his back, advanced to meet the foe. But when he came to the peak of the Mountain of Sand, he beheld in the northern sky a monstrous cloud that drew nearer and ever nearer, and at length he saw that the cloud was no simple cloud but a mighty horde of the wild beasts of the forest. And some were whole, and some were sorely wounded, and bidding his armies halt, he cried to a buzzard that trailed his torn wing behind him: "Whence art thou come and who hath dealt thee this hurt?"

And the buzzard answered: "The Shiraigol hosts that camp on the Chatun Stream have driven us before them as they marched, and harried us with all manner of missiles, slaying many of my comrades and wounding more." So saying, the buzzard departed after his brethren.

And Shumar the Eagle-hero bent his keen gaze upon the Chatun Stream where the enemy was encamped. And he cried aloud: "We may not overcome them, for their numbers are as though the stars of the sky had fallen to earth."

And Nantsong made answer: "Fie upon thee, Shumar! When hast thou seen the stars fall to the earth, that thou shouldst utter such madness! And what though their power be greater than thou canst measure! Is ours so scant?"

And the Lord Shikeer spoke and said: "Youngest of Gessar's heroes though thou be, Nantsong, thy words are sweet with wisdom. If our enemy seethe as a cauldron of boiling milk, let us be as the ladle that empties it—a flood to their flame, a channel to their torrent, and to their arrogance a chastening rod. We will divide our forces in three parts, and I will lead my troops against Tsagan Khan, and bring back the sundered head of each enemy slain. And thou,

Shumar, shalt fall upon Sheera Khan and take his right thumb from the hand of each enemy slain. And Nantsong shall sally forth against Chara Khan, and take his right ear from the head of each enemy slain. And when we have put to rout those that remain, we will return again to the Mountain of Sand."

And they divided their forces in three parts, and placing themselves at the head of their warriors, they cried to their steeds: "Rush like a torrent down the mountainside! Leap like a wolf into the midst of the foe!" And their steeds yawned thrice in answer, and thrice they waved their tails from side to side, and smote their forefeet thrice upon the earth. And they rushed like torrents down the mountainside, and leaped like wolves into the midst of the foe, and all the hosts of Tibet followed after them.

And it was as though their swords had been wrought of flame, and their arrows shot from the bows of angry gods, and as though the earth and heavens spun in terror, so furious was their onslaught. And their chargers snorted columns of dense smoke, so that comrade was hidden from comrade, and they struck the enemies' standards into the dust, and unhorsed their riders and trampled on those afoot.

And the Lord Shikeer slew five hundred thousand men of the armies of Tsagan Khan, and his warriors slew as many. And driving before them the steeds they had taken captive, they withdrew to the Mountain of Sand.

And Shumar the Eagle slew a hundred thousand men of the armies of Sheera Khan, and his warriors slew as many. And driving before them the steeds they had taken captive, they set forth for the Mountain of Sand.

But ere they had journeyed the distance of an arrow's flight, they heard a cry. And turning his head, Shumar saw that a horseman, riding a stallion to whose feet anvils were bound, sought to overtake him. And he wheeled his charger, awaiting the horseman's coming.

And when he was come within six paces of Shumar, the horseman drew rein and cried: "Shumar that art named the Eagle! I am Mergen of the Six Thumbs, who shoots at once six arrows from the bow! And though thou hast slain a hundred thousand men and routed many besides, me thou hast neither slain nor put to rout. Wherefore I charge thee, beggar and thief of Tibet, give back the steeds thou hast stolen, else will I shoot six arrows into thy body and take back thy head in triumph to Sheera Khan!"

"Did I capture thy steeds that I might return them again, thou six-thumbed fool? Begone while yet thou art whole, nor vaunt thy prowess, for thou art no archer but a babe that toys with arrows."

"Wilt thou make trial of thine excellence, O magpie's tongue?"

"That will I. Mark how three eagles soar over yonder mountain. Mark now my arrow's flight!"

And Shumar spanned his bow, and his arrow sped to the foot of the mountain and vanished within, but issuing forth again at the mountain's crest, it soared yet higher, and plunged itself into the breast of each eagle in turn, and brought them to earth. But the arrow returned to Shumar.

And Mergen cried: "I will not challenge thee, for thou hast wrought such wonders as I have never beheld. Yet the peacock takes pride in her tail, and the wise man in his honor, and I dare not return to my master with empty hands. Wherefore I pray thee, give me two chargers of all thou hast taken, a black and a white, and I will depart from thy presence and bless thy name."

"Whether thou bless or curse my name, I care not, Knight of Six Thumbs. But I would know wherefore thy stallion bears an anvil bound to each foot."

"So untamed is his spirit that but for these anvils he would spurn the earth and consort with the wingèd creatures of the air."

"He pleases me. Wherefore do thou deliver him up to me, and I will give thee in payment two chargers, black and white, and seven besides."

"Nay, I will not deliver him up to thee. For how shall I meet my comrades, lacking my steed?"

"And what hinders me from slaying thee and taking thy steed, thou cowardly poltroon? Long since thou shouldst have perished, save that I would have had thee bear to the three Shiraigol Khans the tale of thine encounter with Shumar. But if thou dispute my will, thou shalt feel my power!" And he lifted his spear to strike.

But ere the spear descended, Mergen cried: "Thou art swift to anger as the bird of heaven whose name thou dost bear! Take thou the stallion and give me in payment a black steed and a white, and seven besides."

And so it was done. And Shumar took the stallion to whose feet anvils were bound and withdrew to the Mountain of Sand.

And Nantsong the Falcon, youngest of Gessar's heroes,

136

slew fifty thousand men of the armies of Chara Khan, and his warriors slew as many. And driving before them the steeds they had taken captive, they set forth for the Mountain of Sand.

But Nantsong bethought him of the shining queues that adorned the heads of the slain, and how bravely they might bedeck his dappled steed. And he cried to his chieftains: "Go ye before me to the Mountain of Sand, and I will come after you."

And he returned to the battlefield and severed from the heads of the fallen their shining queues, binding them to the mane and tail of his steed. And Teergen, son of the Khan of Enedkek, beheld Nantsong as he severed the queues and cried: "What knave art thou that thus dishonors our dead?"

"No knave, but the youngest of Gessar's heroes and thy sworn foe."

"Dost thou think to affright me with the name of Gessar, thou puny stripling? Teergen am I, son of the mighty Khan of Enedkek, whose glory dims the light of the sun and moon, and I command thee to return to me the queues thou hast taken."

"Fain would I yield to thy command, save that to please thee were to grieve my steed. Behold how bravely these queues bedeck his beauty."

"Because I honor thy valor, Nantsong, I will parley with thee. See where three wild geese wing their way over the heavens. Should I slay all with one arrow, the queues are mine. Should I fail, thou shalt take them with thee to Tibet."

"Let it be so!"

And Teergen spanned his bow, and aimed his arrow at the wild geese that winged their way through the heavens. But when Nantsong lifted his gaze to follow the flight of the arrow, Teergen sped it against his foe, and it entered one armpit and issued forth from the other, and Nantsong fell to the earth.

But straightway he rose again, and unloosed his girdle, and bound it about his armpits, staunching the black blood's flow. And he cried: "Thou wert not born to slay me, heart of a sheep, but to take death at my hands. My arrow shall pierce thee, leaving thee so much life as will suffice to bear thee back to thy friends. But when thou hast told them how, like a viper, thou didst wound Nantsong, and he, defying death, dealt thee destruction, then perish, Teergen, son of the Khan of Enedkek, whose glory shall be forgotten in thy shame."

And as he said, so did he. And his arrow pierced the skull of his enemy, who faltered and fell. But so much life was left him as sufficed to bear him back to the Shiraigol camp, where, having related the manner of his downfall, he straightway perished.

And Nantsong set forth again for the Mountain of Sand, but his limbs were heavy, and his throat was parched with thirst, and his wounds tore at his arms like the fangs of an adder. And he swayed and would have fallen to the right, but his dappled steed turned his long neck to the right and held him erect in the saddle. And they rode onward, and he swayed and would have fallen to the left, but his dappled steed turned his long neck to the left and held him upright in the saddle. And they rode onward, and now he swayed forward, and though the dappled steed sought to stretch back his neck and uphold his master, he could not, and Nantsong fell from the saddle, and lay bereft of power on the earth.

And two wolves drew nigh that they might feast on his flesh, and two ravens that they might pluck forth his eyes from his head, but the dappled steed stood guard above him and struck at them with his forefeet, snorting black smoke and flame from his nostrils, and when they sought to steal on him from behind, he struck at them with his hindfeet, so that the sparks flew from beneath his hoofs, searing their flesh.

And he cried in sorrow: "Nantsong! Falcon of heaven! Art thou snared indeed! Where are my comrades who were wont to surround me as its feathers surround a bird? Where are thy brothers who were wont to cleave closer one to the other than the leaves of a tree? I may not leave thee to seek them, for the wolves would devour thee and the ravens pluck forth thine eyes. Who then would lay his hand in tenderness upon me, and name me his faithful dappled steed?"

And as he lamented, his eyes lighted upon the ravens that hovered above him, and suddenly he bethought himself and cried: "Birds of ill omen, it will avail you naught to hover above me, for ere I will suffer you to pluck forth the eyes of my master, I will pluck forth your own. But if ye will be my friends and serve my desire, ye shall feast upon the bodies of these wolves in reward for your service."

And the ravens answered: "How may we serve thee, steed of the artful tongue?"

"Fly swiftly to the peak of the Mountain of Sand, and say to the Lord Shikeer that Gessar's Falcon-hero perishes of thirst and a bitter wound in his side."

And the ravens flew swiftly to the peak of the Mountain of Sand, and circling above the head of Shikeer, they cried: "Give heed to our words, lord of the hosts of Tibet! For a dappled steed, artful of tongue and valorous of spirit, bids us say that Gessar's Falcon-hero perishes of thirst and a bitter wound in his side."

And a great cry arose from the throats of the warriors, and drawing their swords from their sheaths, they shouted: "Vengeance! Vengeance on him that hath wounded Nantsong the Falcon!"

But Shikeer lifted up his hand and stilled the clamor and cried: "If the Falcon be wounded, my comrades, doubt not that he who hath dealt the wound is slain, and Nantsong hath more need of healing than of vengeance. Wherefore summon Kinggen the Healer, that he may go with me in search of our brother, and when he hath been made whole of his wound, we will return again."

And Shikeer took Kinggen the Healer behind him upon his saddle, and the wingèd charger followed the flight of the ravens till they came to the spot where Nantsong the Falcon lay, bereft of power. And his dappled steed stood guard above him, and the tears flowed from his eyes.

But when he beheld Shikeer, he checked his weeping and fell upon the wolves that had harried him, and rent them limb from limb. And the ravens feasted upon their flesh.

And Kinggen the Healer poured the juices of fragrant

herbs into the wounds of Nantsong and made him whole, and rising refreshed, he mounted his dappled steed, and so they journeyed back to the Mountain of Sand.

And when his comrades beheld Nantsong, they laughed for joy, and when they beheld his steed, bedecked with the shining queues of the enemy, their laughter echoed to the camp of the three Shiraigol Khans who trembled to hear it.

But suddenly Shumar the Eagle cried: "Two riders gallop toward us, and one is the Lady Rogmo, and one is the Prince Chotong who follows after her."

And the riders drew nigh, and having scaled the Mountain of Sand and reached its summit, the Lady Rogmo cried: "I am come to join you, for it ill beseems the chosen wife of Gessar to bide at home, awaiting the battle's issue. But wherefore Chotong hath followed me I know not, for he is come by his own will and not by mine."

And Chotong cried: "I feared for the safety of the Lady Rogmo, and therefore I followed her."

But Shikeer answered him: "For whose safety didst thou fear, Chotong, when thou didst counsel her to flee to some lonely isle in the Chatun Stream, that the Shiraigol Khans might leave thee unmolested? Nay, thou art come to share our spoils, having shunned our perils. But though we have captured a mighty horde of steeds, there is none for thee. Nine chosen herds must be offered up in thanksgiving to the gods, and nine must be paid in tribute to the Lady Rogmo, and when the thirty heroes have taken their share, and all our warriors have been rewarded, and a steed bestowed on those who now go afoot, what will be left for thee, daunt-

141

less Chotong, save to return on the nag that bore thee hither?" And Chotong was angered by the words of Shikeer, but the warriors laughed.

And when nine chosen herds had been offered up in thanksgiving to the gods, and nine had been paid in tribute to the Lady Rogmo, those that remained were allotted among the thirty heroes and the chieftains and warriors of the three tribes of Tibet, and a steed was bestowed on those who went afoot. And Shumar the Eagle gave to the Lord Shikeer the tireless stallion he had taken from Mergen of the Six Thumbs, that he might be a comrade to the wingèd charger. But no steed of all the treasure was given to Chotong.

And night fell upon the peak of the Mountain of Sand, and the armies slumbered.

VII. THE TREACHERY OF CHOTONG

O F THE TREACHERY OF THE VILE CHOTONG,
WHEREBY THE THREE SHIRAIGOL KHANS
WERE ENABLED TO SEIZE THE BEAUTEOUS
LADY ROGMO AND BEAR HER INTO CAPTIVITY.

But Chotong slumbered not, for his anger writhed as
a serpent within his breast. And he thought: "No steed of
all their treasure have they allotted me. Therefore I will
descend the mountain and, screened by the night, I will
plunder the enemy's herds and, when I return, I will flaunt

my booty before Shikeer who hath made a mock of me. But naught of my spoils will I bestow upon him or upon his comrades."

And he stole down the slope of the Mountain of Sand to the enemy's camp, and screened by the darkness, he plundered their herds, then driving his booty before him, set forth again for the tents of his countrymen.

But one who was named Ulan of the Red Eyes espied him as he journeyed over the plain, and rode in pursuit. And Chotong, hearing the galloping hoofbeats behind him, leaped from his steed and sought shelter within a woodrat's narrow lair. And Ulan of the Red Eyes drew rein before the lair and cried: "Come forth, thou wondrous woodrat that plunders the herds of men!"

And Chotong answered: "The herds are thine, Shiraigol knight! Take them and my steed as well, but leave me within the shelter of this lair, for I am an ancient man and cannot serve thee."

"Nay, since thou art so lavish of thy bounty with herd and steed, I would have thy sword as well and thy bow and arrows. Come forth straightway, else will I kindle such a blaze before thy lair as will drive thee forth, whether living or dead I care not!"

And Chotong crept forth, and Ulan of the Red Eyes bound him hand and foot, and flinging him over his saddle, returned with him to the Shiraigol camp. And at dawn he led Chotong before his masters, and recounted the manner of his capture.

And Chotong lay prone before the Shiraigol Khans,

146

and besought them piteously, crying: "Grant me my life, ye most glorious among the sovereigns of earth, and I will reveal to you how ye may win the victory over your foe, and take the Lady Rogmo captive."

And Tsagan Khan ordered that Chotong be released from his bonds, and when he had been released, he bowed nine times to the ground, striking his palms nine times upon one another. Then laying his brow on the feet of Tsagan Khan, he awaited his word.

And Tsagan Khan cried: "Arise, Chotong, and say what thou art minded to say!"

And Chotong arose and spoke: "Though Gessar's heroes are mighty beyond all men, and not to be equalled in the arts of war, through guile ye may overcome them. Therefore return to me my armor and my weapons and my steed, and give me as well some score of your own steeds that have passed their prime, and I will go to my countrymen and say: 'The Shiraigol Khans have withdrawn from the Chatun Stream and journey homeward. I followed in their wake, but so swift was their retreat that I might not overtake them, and coming upon these steeds that they had abandoned, I drove them hither.' Hearing these tidings, Shikeer will disband his armies and return to his home on the Stream of the Elephant, but the Lady Rogmo will prepare a feast for the thirty heroes in honor of their victory. Having drunk deeply, they will slumber deeply, and in that hour ye may safely send your forces to take the Lady Rogmo captive."

And Tsagan Khan rejoiced in the counsel of Chotong,

and commanded that his armor be returned to him and his weapons and his steed, and that he be given some score of their own steeds that had passed their prime. And driving this herd before him, Chotong set forth again for the Mountain of Sand.

And when he had reached the peak, Shikeer and the thirty heroes greeted him, crying: "Welcome, Chotong! What sorry array of steeds is this that bears thee company?"

And Chotong answered: "The Shiraigol Khans are withdrawn from the Chatun Stream and, humbled in defeat, they journey homeward. I followed after them, hoping to take captive a herd of steeds, since ye would give me naught of all your treasure. Yet so swift was their retreat that I might not overtake them, and coming upon these steeds that they had abandoned, I drove them hither, lest ye doubt the truth of my tidings."

"Art thou our foe that we should doubt thy tidings? Comrades, Chotong our kinsman brings us word that the Shiraigol Khans are withdrawn from the Chatun Stream and journey homeward. Wherefore let us disband our hosts and return to our dwelling-places!"

But the Lady Rogmo cried: "Shikeer, I pray thee, take heed! How often hath Gessar warned us: 'The voice of Chotong is soft as the rarest of silks, his words are sweet as the richest of fine cakes, but his heart is harder than the hardest flint.' Trust not his tidings, Shikeer, for he is a liar whose like the golden sun hath never beheld!"

"A liar he is and a coward, Lady Rogmo, yet when hath he betrayed us, that we should charge him with so foul a

deed? Nay, he speaks truly! Wherefore let us disband our hosts, and return in peace to our dwelling-places!"

And the hosts were disbanded, and Shikeer returned to the Stream of the Elephant, but the thirty heroes, riding on either hand of the Lady Rogmo, brought her in triumph to her yurta.

And she ordered that a feast be prepared in honor of their victory, and they ate abundantly of the flesh of oxen and of boars, and drank deep draughts of potent brandy, and at dawn they slumbered.

But the Lady Rogmo said to Arigon, her servant: "Ride forth, my Arigon, and bring me tidings if the Shiraigol Khans be indeed departed, for my soul is beset with fears."

And Arigon rode forth, but ere he had crossed two streams, he beheld the Shiraigol hosts advancing toward him. And he would have turned to sound the alarm, but an enemy's arrow pierced his breast, and he fell from his steed and perished.

And the hostile forces crept silently upon the slumbering heroes of Tibet, their swords unsheathed. And the Lady Rogmo, awaiting the tidings of Arigon, espied them from the doorway of her yurta and uttered a piercing cry.

And the heroes awoke, but their eyes were heavy with sleep and their limbs with drinking, and the strength of thirty was less than the strength of one. And they sought to summon their steeds that grazed in a distant pasture, but though each steed answered the summons with a loud neighing, they could not break the ranks of the enemy that held them from their masters.

And the heroes fought on foot, and their swords flashed, and their arrows sped to the mark, and their spears were plunged into the breasts of the foe, and each hero slew fifty thousand men of the Shiraigol hosts. But Chara Khan leaned from his saddle, and thrust his spear through the breast of the Tiger-hero, and the Tiger-hero fell to earth and perished.

And Sheera Khan urged his steed against Nantsong, who was engaged in combat with a thousand men, and the steed rode him down and trampled upon him, and when he would have risen, Sheera Khan plunged his sword into the throat of Nantsong and slew him.

And Tsagan Khan sent his arrow against Shumar, who seized it to turn it from his breast. But the point, that was envenomed, pierced his hand, and he swayed and fell. And Tsagan Khan smote his head from his shoulders, and he perished.

And all the heroes of Gessar perished save Bodotshi, who was named the Fire-hero, for upon him the gods had bestowed the power to transform himself to flame. And now as a burning coal he rolled through the enemy's lines, and those whom his breath touched were consumed to ashes. And the earth over which he passed was a lake of fire, and those that stood upon it were engulfed in its depths. And none could approach Bodotshi to slay him, nor quench his heat, but so fiercely did he rage to destroy the foe that at length he was consumed in his own fires.

And the Lady Rogmo beheld with a sorrowing heart the slaughter of Gessar's heroes, but when she saw that none remained to defend her, she withdrew into her yurta, and laid beneath her robe a sabre forged of unbending steel, and girded a bow and quiver about her shoulders, with a hundred golden arrows whereon Gessar had cast a potent spell ere he set forth for the country of the twelve-headed giant. And she cried: "Because the son of heaven tarries in distant realms, and Shikeer, unheedful of my warning, is departed to the Stream of the Elephant, and the thirty heroes have yielded up their lives in my service, shall I sit idly by and weep, awaiting the coming of the foe? Nay, I will go forth and do battle with him!"

And she went forth, and forty chieftains advanced to meet her, checking their steeds to a soft and sober pace, lest the dust stirred by their hoofs should sully the countenance of the Lady Rogmo.

And Rogmo questioned them, crying: "Ye valiant ones that come to take me captive, are ye chieftains in your land or simple tribesmen?"

And they answered: "We are chieftains in our land."

"It is well. Do ye range yourselves in a single rank before me, and I will go at your head, and so deliver myself up to the Khans of Shiraigol."

And they ranged themselves in a single rank before her, and she placed herself at their head. But ere they could read her purpose, she had sped a golden arrow from her bow that pierced the breast of each chieftain in turn, tumbling them from their steeds and stretching them lifeless upon the earth.

And mounting the foremost steed, she galloped into the

midst of the foe, and her arrows fell like a golden rain among them, and so potent was Gessar's spell that each arrow slew a thousand warriors ere it sank earthward like a wounded bird and was still. And those that escaped the arrows were hurled into confusion, for comrade grappled with comrade, and frenzied steeds trampled their riders to death beneath their heels, and terror reigned among the Shiraigol hosts seeking to flee the fury of the Lady Rogmo.

But Tsagan Khan lifted up his voice above the din of battle and cried: "Are ye men or geese that ye flee from the wrath of a woman? Stand fast and surround her, for by the head of my sire I swear that whoso defies my command shall die at the point of my sabre!"

And the three Shiraigol Khans rode up and down among the affrighted armies, restoring their ranks to order. And they surrounded the Lady Rogmo, whose quiver was empty of all save a single arrow, husbanded against her direst need. And from beneath her robe she drew forth the sabre of unbending steel and laid about her, slashing to right and left, and unhorsing a thousand riders at each blow. But now they pressed upon her from every hand, and she could neither escape through their serried lines nor wield her weapon. And she transformed herself into a wasp and rose above them, but Tsagan Khan transformed himself into a snowy hawk, and Sheera Khan into a yellow hawk, and Chara Khan into a sable hawk, and they pursued her and drove her back to earth. And all her arts being spent, she yielded to them.

Thus was the Lady Rogmo taken captive by the three Khans of Shiraigol.

And they mounted her upon a blue-black steed that bore her proudly, and set forth for their domain. And Rogmo plucked a hair from her eyebrow and laid it in the palm of her white hand, and spoke to it softly, saying: "Go with the wind to the Stream of the Elephant, and bear the tidings of my plight to the Lord Shikeer!"

And the hair went with the wind to the Stream of the Elephant, and entered the nostril of Shikeer, so that he sneezed and cried: "What is thy message, hair of the Lady Rogmo?"

And the hair replied: "Chotong hath betrayed thee, and the Shiraigol Khans have slain the thirty heroes and taken the Lady Rogmo captive."

And Shikeer leaped to his wingèd charger, and rode to the yurta of Sanglun on the Lion's Stream. And he cried: "I go to take vengeance upon the Shiraigol Khans, who have slain the thirty heroes and taken the Lady Rogmo captive."

And Sanglun cried: "Whose power hath wrought this evil?"

And Shikeer made answer: "The power of the treachery of Chotong!"

And Sanglun said: "My son, the past lies far behind me, but that which is to come lies near at hand. Wherefore I will gird on my armor and go into battle by thy side."

"Nay, sire, for thou art as an oak blasted by many storms, whose boughs are withered and whose sap flows sluggishly in its veins. Do thou bide here and await the coming of Gessar, lest there be none to welcome his return."

"My bones are withered indeed, and my blood flows sluggishly, and the storms of many years have blasted my frame. I would fain have known the joy of death in battle, but since thou hast said: 'Thy strength is spent, Sanglun! Bide thou the coming of Gessar!' I answer: My strength is spent, Shikeer, and as thou hast decreed it, I will bide here the coming of Gessar Khan!"

And Shikeer bade his sire farewell, and gave rein to his wingèd charger, crying: "Bear me to the peak of the Mountain of Sand, from whose height I may look down on the retreating hosts, and tell over their number!"

And the wingèd charger leaped forward, and brought his master soon to the Mountain of Sand, from whose height he looked down upon the retreating hosts, and saw that their number was four hundred thousand, and in their midst, mounted upon a blue-black steed, he beheld the Lady Rogmo.

And his heart was oppressed with woe and he cried: "How shall I answer my brother when he returns and says: 'What hast thou done, Shikeer?' Shall I answer him: 'Because I was unheedful of thy word, and the word of the Lady Rogmo, therefore are thy thirty heroes slain, and thy chosen wife a captive in the land of the Shiraigol Khans!' Nay, rather will I plunge down among them, to slay and be slain, for what worth has my life to me, lacking Gessar's love?"

And Rogmo heard his words and cried to him: "Shikeer! Hawk among men! Though the tree be shattered, do not the roots remain? Though the man perish, doth not his seed live after him? Despair not, but seek out Gessar, for alone thou shalt not prevail over this enemy, and he will restore to life the thirty heroes, and together ye shall take vengeance on those that have wronged him!"

And Shikeer made answer: "Wilt thou veil thy countenance from thy captors' gaze till I am returned again with Gessar Khan?"

And she replied: "For a twelvemonth will I veil my countenance from my captors' gaze, but when that time is past, I must needs wed with the Prince Gereltu. Make haste, therefore, Shikeer! Make haste, thou wingèd charger! Leap like a wild goat over the mountain peaks, swim through the waters like the king of fish, outspeed the rushing winds that sweep the heavens, and bring me succor!"

And Shikeer would have turned his steed to do her bidding, but Tsagan Khan taunted him, crying: "Valiant Shikeer! Faithful friend to thy master! What wilt thou say to Gessar when thou hast found him? Wilt thou say: 'The thirty heroes have perished in defense of the Lady Rogmo, but I abandoned her to her captors and went in search of thee, for I feared to challenge them to battle single-handed, lest they should do me harm!'"

And the rage of Shikeer was inflamed by his enemy's taunt, and his eyes rolled in his head. And drawing forth his sabre from its sheath, he whetted the keen edge upon a flint, then smote his wingèd charger a mighty blow and leaped from the mountain peak to the plain beneath him.

And he mowed down the Shiraigol hosts as a reaper mows down a field of grain, and he dealt with them as an axe deals

156

with the forest. And the Chatun Stream was choked with the bodies of the slain, and her waters ran red with their blood.

And Shikeer, having slaughtered seventy thousand men, sought out their leader. And he cried: "Where dost thou lurk, Tsagan, thou loud of tongue but timorous of deed? Come forth, and measure thy might against Shikeer's, that all thy warriors may know at length what manner of craven leads them!"

And Tsagan Khan came forth to meet Shikeer, but when his tireless steed and the wingèd charger looked upon one another, they whinneyed in joy, for they were near akin, and in their youth had gamboled in one pasture. And now they would not contend against one another, but when their riders urged them on, they retreated, and though the lash flayed their shoulders and the spurs their thighs, the steeds defied the bidding of their masters, and went not forward, but back.

And Shikeer thought: "I will alight and slake my thirst at the Chatun Stream, for my labors have wearied me. And being restored to the freshness of my strength, I will bend this steed to my will."

And he alighted, that he might slake his thirst at the Chatun Stream, but its waters were defiled with his enemy's blood, and scarcely had he laid his lips against them when he fell in a deep swoon upon the bank.

And Tsagan Khan, seeking a means whereby he might undo his foe, dismounted and hewed down a mighty pine that crashed across the throat of Shikeer and was like to strangle him. But the wingèd charger, fondling him with his tongue, awakened him, and he strove to arise but could not, nor could he move his head to left or right. And Tsagan Khan bore down upon him with a drawn sword.

But now a hawk swooped from the heavens and hovered above Shikeer, and as the sword descended, smiting his head from his shoulders, the life of Shikeer departed from his body and entered into the body of the hawk, who soared aloft into the blue heavens and vanished.

VIII. THE PUNISHMENT OF THE THREE SHIRAIGOL KHANS

OF GESSAR KHAN'S DEPARTURE FROM THE COUNTRY OF THE TWELVE-HEADED GIANT, AND HOW HE OVERTHREW HIS ENEMIES, AND SUCCORED THE BEAUTEOUS LADY ROGMO.

And as the Lady Rogmo journeyed in the midst of her captors, she drew forth from her quiver the golden arrow, husbanded against her direst need. And she plucked a feather from its plumage, and pricked her wrist with its point, then wrote in her blood upon the arrow's shaft a message to Gessar Khan. And she spoke to the arrow,

163

saying: "Thou dart of gold that Gessar's hand hath blessed, seek out thy master!" And hurling it from her, she continued on her way to the realm of the Shiraigol Khans.

Now Gessar took his ease upon the wall of the giant's castle, and the Lady Aralgo sat by his side. For she feared to leave him, lest one should come and impart to him the tale of her evil doing. And when he walked abroad, she bore him company; and when he tarried within, she was ever nigh.

But the brown wonder-steed lay pent in a deep dungeon, whither she had enticed him with oats and golden wheat to follow her. And she had fettered his legs with gyves of iron, and weighted his neck with an iron halter, and bound him fast to an iron beam, and sealed the dungeon gate. And for many moons he lay without food or drink, but each twelvemonth, when the snows melted and the streams were released from bondage, she entered his dungeon and scattered a handful of hay, that he might eat, and gave him a cup of water to quench his thirst, then left him to languish for another twelvemonth.

Now as she sat with Gessar on the castle wall, he said: "The midday sun beats fiercely about my head. Go thou within and prepare a cooling draught, that I may be refreshed."

But scarcely was she departed, when an ancient crone appeared on the path below him, driving an ancient cow before her.

And Gessar cried: "Good mother, wherefore dost thou drive this hoary beast to pasture? Surely she hath served thee well and earned release from labor, for her horns are crumbling with age."

And the crone answered: "Nine weary years hath she served me, having been a calf when Gessar Khan vanquished the twelve-headed giant. Yet she is doomed to labor till the charm that holds him here be lifted." And the crone went her way, but the heart of Gessar was troubled by her words.

And now a rook flew from the east, alighting on the path below him, and Gessar cried: "Is thy land barren of food, O hungering rook, that thou art come hither to forage?"

And the rook answered: "The land of my birth lies to the east of this castle, near the Black Pyramid, and ever it hath been my wont to fly to the west in search of food for my mate and my fledglings. Yet when night comes down, I return to them again, that I may guard them from harm. Far otherwise hast thou dealt with those that love thee, all-conquering one whom Aralgo's wiles have conquered. Where is the Lady Rogmo, thy beauteous wife? Where is Shikeer, the brother of thy heart? Where are the thirty heroes and all thy people who have looked to thee for comfort? Since thou hast thought it well to abandon them to death and captivity, meeter it were that thou withhold thy scorn from those that obey Buddha's law."

And the rook went his way, but the spirit of Gessar was in turmoil, as when an angry wind sweeps through the branches of a tree, shattering its peace.

And now the enchanted arrow appeared in the blue heavens, winging its way to Gessar. And marking him

165

where he sat upon the castle wall, the dart descended and came to rest within his empty quiver. And Gessar drew it forth and read upon its shaft the word of the Lady Rogmo: "Dost thou live, Gessar? Then know that thy brother Shikeer is vanished from the earth, and thy thirty heroes lie slain on the battlefield through the treachery of the vile Chotong, and Rogmo, thy chosen wife, is taken captive by the three Shiraigol Khans. If thou be in life, deliver me from their bondage, but if thou be overthrown by the giant's might or the craft of the Lady Aralgo, I will bare my countenance to the gaze of my captors and wed with the Prince Gereltu."

And the darkness wherein for nine weary years he had lain was lifted from Gessar, and he cried: "How have I wronged thee, Shikeer my brother, and my thirty heroes, and Rogmo, my peerless wife!" And so bitterly did he weep that the sound of his lamentations reached even unto the ears of the brown wonder-steed, and multiplied his rage a hundredfold, and as his rage increased so did his power, until his strength was as the strength of thirteen dragons. And he tore himself from the iron beam that held him, and flung the iron halter from his shoulders, and rent the iron fetters from his legs, and crashed through the dungeon gate. And with a mighty roar he approached his master and cried: "Thy noble brother is vanished, thy thirty heroes are slain, thy chosen wife is captured, and all to content the Lady Aralgo! Yet now that thy wits have been restored to thee, canst thou do naught save howl like a beaten slave to the high heavens?" So saying, he turned his back upon the castle and fled away.

And Gessar cried: "Return to me, wonder-steed, for the gods have endowed thee with wisdom, but I am a fool!"

But the steed came not to his summons, and Gessar cried: "My glorious sisters, capture my steed and lead him back to me, for without him I may not escape from this land of woe!"

And the voice of his sisters sounded from Sumeru: "He will not return, for thou hast offended him. But mount whatsoever steed thou shalt find in the giant's stables, and follow after, and it may be thou shalt woo him from his anger."

And Gessar found in the stables of the giant his copper-green mule, and leading him forth, he cried to Aralgo: "Thou artful one that hast brought me to dishonor! Give me my helmet and mine armor and my spear, that I may depart out of this land of woe!"

And thrusting her head from the casement, Aralgo cried: "What helmet and what armor and what spear, thou beggar out of Tibet on a stunted steed! Curst be that day of sorrow that saw thee slay my gentle husband, the twelve-headed giant, who would have sheltered me from thine ill usage!"

And Gessar answered naught, but opening wide his jaws, sent forth a cry that rocked the earth, and eight and eighty times the giant's castle spun round and round, then burst into raging flame.

And Aralgo flung from the casement his helmet and his

armor and his spear, and Gessar cried to the flames: "Let her issue forth unscathed!" And she issued forth, but the castle was consumed to ashes.

And when Gessar had donned his armor, he mounted the copper-green mule, and seating the Lady Aralgo behind him, descended the lofty peak. And the bones of the giants that had guarded the ebon ridge lay mouldering in the dust, but the sons of men that had watched the golden ridge, and the sons of the gods that had kept the pearly ridge were long departed out of the giant's realm.

And when Gessar had journeyed for a night and a day and an hour, he came upon a herd of chigitai, and in their midst crouched the brown wonder-steed, seeking to hide from his sight.

And Gessar cried: "Ho, thou brown wonder-steed! Wilt thou come to my call, or shall I shoot thy four legs from thy hoofs and leave thee to perish?"

And the brown wonder-steed went forth from the midst of the herd, and laying his head against his master's hand, he spoke.

"When I dwelt with thee in Tibet, the Lady Rogmo adorned me with trappings of silk, and fashioned of gold the buckles of my harness, and laid a velvet cushion beneath my saddle, lest my coat be marred. In winter she decked me with the skins of sables, in summer she led me into shady groves from whose waters I might drink. At dawn and noon and nightfall she fed me with oats and golden wheat, and often when ye feasted she brought me almonds and sugar from your board, and other foods pleasant to men and

steeds. But I was parted from her, and from Shikeer and the thirty heroes, and from my comrades whom I loved well, and the Lady Aralgo cast me into a dungeon, and bound me with gyves of iron, and left me to languish for nine weary years, hungering and athirst. Therefore was my anger kindled against thee, dear master, for my wrongs were greater than I could bear."

And Gessar answered: "Thine anger is just, and thy wrongs shall be avenged!" And mounting his wonder-steed, he turned his head toward the Shiraigol realm that lay to the north. And the Lady Aralgo followed after him on the copper-green mule.

And presently she cried: "I hunger!" And Gessar flung her a stirrup of leather and answered: "For one that hungers, here is toothsome food!"

"No food is this, but a stirrup of foul leather!"

"Nay, eat, for it is the flesh of a wondrous ox!"

And Aralgo took the stirrup into her mouth, but spat it forth again, crying in wrath: "Evil it is to the taste as to the sight!"

And they rode farther, and presently she cried: "I thirst!" And Gessar pointed out the bed of a stream whose waters the sun had drunk, and answered: "For one that thirsts, here are cooling waters!"

"I see no waters, but a bed of mire!"

"Nay, drink, for they are the waters of an enchanted stream!"

And Aralgo took the mire into her mouth but spat it forth again, crying in wrath: "Wherefore dost thou give me leathern stirrups to eat, and mire to quench my thirst?"

"That the wrongs of my wonder-steed may be avenged, and thine evil deeds requited. And for the draught of forgetfulness whereby thou didst enslave the son of heaven, thou shalt come no more to the Valley of Pleasant Winds but wander through the Lonely Desert till thy years be spent!"

And straightway the Lady Aralgo was transported to the Lonely Desert, where she wandered till her years were spent, but Gessar continued on his way to the realm of the Shiraigol Khans.

And as he rode through the wilderness, a voice rang forth: "Stay, Gessar!"

And he cried: "Who calls upon my name? Neither man nor bird nor dog inhabits this wilderness, yet surely one cried out: 'Stay, Gessar!'"

But no answer came, and he would have ridden farther, yet when he spurred his steed forward again, again the voice rang forth: "Stay, Gessar!"

And he peered on every hand and before and behind him, and at length he raised his eyes to the heavens and beheld a creature whose head was as the head of a man, but whose body and tail were fashioned like a hawk's. And the creature flew earthward and alighted on his saddle-bow.

And he cried: "All-conquering, all-healing Gessar Khan! I am Shikeer thy brother, and since my head was smitten from my body at the Chatun Stream, I have awaited thy coming."

And Gessar uttered a mighty cry and embraced his

brother, and they wept so that the earth shook with their weeping, and the mountains and forest wept to see their grief.

But when their tears were spent, Gessar scattered incense upon the earth, stilling its tumult, and cried: "Let us have done with sorrow! And I will make sacrifice to Kormuzda my father, and entreat him to restore thee again to mortal form."

And Shikeer made answer: "Entreat him not, Gessar, for whether I would be restored again to mortal form I know not. But till thou have made an end of him that vanquished me through the felling of a pine and of all his kin, my spirit may not find repose in heaven or on earth."

And Gessar cried: "Then farewell, Shikeer, for I go to win repose for thy spirit." And taking leave of his brother, he galloped onward.

And when he was come within three days' journey of the Shiraigol borders, he drew from his quiver the enchanted arrow that the Lady Rogmo had sent him. And he cried: "Go thou before me, and destroy the sentinels that guard the borders, lest they herald my coming to my foe!" And leaping from his hand, the arrow took its flight to Shiraigol.

Now the sentinels that guarded the borders of the kingdom were three. And the first could see farther than a falcon can fly in three days, and the second could hear farther than a fox can run in three days, and the third could reach farther than an army can march in three days.

And the Far-Seeing One cried to his comrades: "What creature is this that comes in flight against us? Is it an eagle? Can it be a raven? Swiftly it nears us, yet its shape is hidden from my sight."

And the Far-Hearing One answered: "It is neither an eagle nor a raven in flight against us, but I hear the singing of an arrow that is fraught with peril to our lives!"

Then the Far-Reaching One spoke to them, saying: "Fear naught, my comrades, but do as I shall bid you, and all will yet be well. Let the Far-Hearing One take shelter behind me, his arms clasped round my waist. And as I shield him, even so let him shield the Far-Seeing One. Thus will we await the arrow's coming, and ere it can do us harm, I will pluck it forth out of the firmament and break it asunder."

And they did as the Far-Reaching One commanded, and when he espied the arrow, he plucked it forth out of the firmament and strove to break it asunder. But he could not, and the arrow bore him aloft, together with his comrades who clung behind him, then plunged with them into a rushing river and left them there to perish. And when Gessar came to the borders of Shiraigol, his arrow awaited him on the river's bank, its head thrust through the mire, its golden plumage shining in the sun.

And Gessar laid it into his quiver and journeyed farther, till he came within sight of the castle of the three Shiraigol Khans. And he halted in the shade of a pleasant grove, where a spring gushed forth, and transforming himself into an aged lama and his steed into a beggar's oaken staff, he laid him down beside the spring as if in slumber.

Now in the cool of the day the daughters of the three

Shiraigol Khans took their way hither, that they might disport themselves in the shade of the trees and drink of the spring's clear water. And they tossed a scarlet fruit from hand to hand, and the Lady Rogmo followed after them, her countenance veiled from sight.

And the scarlet fruit fell from the hands of a maid into the lama's mouth as he lay by the spring. And they ran to his side and berated him, crying: "Who art thou, graybeard, that hast dared to enter the grove of the three Khans' daughters, and snatch our scarlet fruit into thy mouth?"

And the lama answered: "Alas, my children, I am a holy man, and I go in search of peace. Of your charity, take not the fruit from my mouth, but suffer me to eat of it, and should it please you to bow your heads before me, I will bless you in Buddha's name."

But the maidens mocked him, crying: "Shall the daughters of a Khan bow down before an unclean beggar?"

And now the Lady Rogmo drew nigh and questioned the lama, saying: "Whence art thou, ancient man, and whither dost thou journey?"

"I journey from foe to friend by way of this land. But I would tarry a little, for my limbs are weary. And because I hunger, I would eat of this scarlet fruit."

And the Lady Rogmo knew him by his words for Gessar Khan, and she cried: "For shame, ye maidens! Would ye wrest from the lips of a holy man the fruit the gods have laid there? Go, slake your thirst at the spring as ye are wont, then depart, and trouble him no more!"

And the maidens did her bidding, and when they were

174

departed, Rogmo cried: "Thou art no ancient lama, but Gessar Khan, son of Kormuzda and my well-loved lord."

And Gessar answered: "Unveil thy countenance, that I may know thee truly for the Lady Rogmo."

And Rogmo unveiled her countenance, and it was as though the sun and the moon and the stars lighted the grove.

And Gessar embraced her, saying: "The enchanted arrow that hath faithfully served us will bear thee now to the bank of the Chatun Stream, and when I have taken vengeance upon thy captors, I will seek thee there."

And the enchanted arrow leaped from his quiver and spread its plumage, making a pleasant couch for the Lady Rogmo, and seated upon it, she was swiftly borne to the bank of the Chatun Stream.

But Gessar released from beneath him a golden spider that was as large as a calf in its second year. And the spider scaled the wall of the castle and encircled it, crying: "Let him that slew the Tiger-hero tremble, for the day of his downfall is at hand!"

And again he encircled the wall of the castle, crying: "Let him that slew Nantsong the Falcon tremble, for the day of his downfall is at hand!"

And a third time he encircled the wall of the castle, crying: "Let him that slew Shumar the Eagle tremble, for the day of his downfall is at hand!" And having encircled the wall of the castle thrice, the spider vanished.

And Tsagan Khan was seated upon his throne, and his second brother sat at his right hand, and his youngest brother at his left. And hearing the cry of the spider, he summoned

175

his sentinels before him, and questioned them, saying: "What man was he that thrice encircled the wall of the castle, uttering a strange cry?"

And the sentinels answered: "No man, nor yet a wild beast of the forest, nor a gentle beast of the fields, but a hornèd creature whose like we have never seen that cried in a mortal's voice."

And the three Khans of Shiraigol trembled, for they knew that Gessar was come from the land of the twelve-headed giant to take vengeance upon them.

But Tsagan Khan cried: "Let ten thousand of our good-liest warriors assemble in the castle court, and let them go forth to do battle with this insolent one that dares send his messenger of evil to the Shiraigol Khans."

And ten thousand warriors assembled in the castle court, but ere they could go forth in search of the enemy, a sword of lightning pierced the rampart, slaying a thousand. And those that remained were hurled into confusion, and here they sought to retreat and there to press forward, but again the sword of lightning cleft the wall, slaying a second thousand. And twice five times the sword flashed in their midst, and ere it vanished the bodies of ten thousand lay lifeless in the castle court.

And mounted on his wonder-steed, Gessar leaped to the wall. And a rainbow encircled his head, and his jeweled armor burned as a living flame, and from the nostrils of his steed black clouds of smoke and yellow tongues of fire ascended to the skies. And brandishing his lightning-sword, he cried: "Wherein did I wrong you, ye lords of Shiraigol, that ye must needs invade my realm, and slay my heroes, and scatter my people over the earth, and take captive my chosen wife?"

And the voice of Tsagan Khan cried from within the castle: "We will restore to thee thy chosen wife!"

"And what of my heroes, whose bones lie bleaching on the field where ye struck them down? Will ye restore my heroes as well?"

"Nay, for how can we give life again to the lifeless?"

"Then, if ye be warriors, come forth and do battle with me! For if ye will not, I will seek you out in your hiding place and slay you."

"We will do battle with thee, Gessar, and as we vanquished thy heroes, so shalt thou be vanquished!"

"Let the gods judge!"

And Tsagan Khan sallied forth on his tireless steed and Gessar leaped down from the rampart to confront him. And he cried: "Do thou ride from the east and I will come from the west, and in this place let our naked swords clash upon one another, sealing our fate."

And one rode from the east and one from the west, and in the place that Gessar had appointed their naked blades clashed upon one another. But Gessar's lightning-sword cleft the sword of his enemy in twain and pierced his breast. And he fell to the earth and his spirit left his body and was seized by shimnus.

And now Sheera Khan issued forth from the castle, and his bow was girded about his shoulders, and his quiver hung by his side.

And Gessar cried: "Wilt thou slay me with an arrow, Sheera Khan?"

And he answered: "I will."

"Then shoot as a skilful marksman, and as a hero I will abide thy shot!"

And Sheera Khan took aim, but Gessar raised his arm and the arrow passed beneath it, lodging in the wall behind him.

Then Gessar fitted an arrow to his bow and let it fly. And the arrow pierced the brow of his enemy, and he fell to the earth, and his spirit left his body.

And now the youngest of the Shiraigol Khans came forth from the castle, and he bore neither sword nor spear, and no bow was girded about his shoulders, and no quiver hung by his side.

And Gessar cried: "Dost thou come to slay or be slain, thou youngest of the Shiraigol Khans?"

"Neither to slay nor be slain, Gessar, but to meet my fate. For shall I seek to escape thee that have overthrown my elder brothers in combat? But since I count a warrior's death sweeter than the flight of a craven, I am come to measure the strength of mine arm against thee."

"Alas, to win peace for the soul of my brother I must slay thee, brave youth! Else were I fain to spare thee for thy valiant heart. Come, try thy strength against me!"

And Gessar alighted from his steed and Chara Khan grappled with him, striving to force him to earth, or fling him over his head, or crush his bones in the cruel embrace of death. But Gessar stood steadfast as a column that is driven

many fathoms into the ground, and his bones were as the tusks of an elephant, and the strength of his enemy availed not against him.

And having striven in vain to overthrow him, Chara Khan cried: "Try now thy strength against me!" And Gessar clasped him and raised him above his head and dashed him with such might to the earth that all his bones were shattered and the crimson blood flowed from a score of wounds. And his spirit left his body and departed to the kingdom of Erleek Khan.

And Gessar, having taken vengeance upon the three Shiraigol Khans, withdrew from their land, and galloped to the bank of the Chatun Stream where the Lady Rogmo awaited him. And she mounted behind him on the brown wonder-steed and they journeyed to Tibet.

IX. THE RETURN OF GESSAR KHAN

OF THE PUNISHMENT METED OUT BY GESSAR
TO THE TRAITOR CHOTONG AND HOW THE
SON OF HEAVEN RETURNED TO RULE OVER
HIS PEOPLE IN THE JOY AND WISDOM OF THE GODS.

Now the brown wonder-steed bore Gessar and the Lady
Rogmo swiftly into Tibet, but when they were come again
within its borders, Gessar transformed himself into a merchant, and the wonder-steed into a lowly ass, and the Lady
Rogmo into a servingman that led his beast by the reins.

And they encountered a herdsman among his flocks, and Gessar cried: "Who is the lord over this fair domain, and what place doth he inhabit?"

And the herdsman answered: "The vile Chotong inhabits the yurta of the mighty Gessar and sits on his throne. Peace hath made way for strife, and gladness for weeping, and his people curse the day when Gessar forsook them to do battle with the twelve-headed giant."

And they fared farther till they came within sight of Gessar's yurta, wherein Chotong dwelt. And Gessar alighted and strewed incense upon the earth, and straightway the plains were thronged with lusty cattle, and bearded goats leaped on the mountainside. And here and there white yurtas blossomed till forty gleamed in the sun, and in their midst, supported on golden arrows, rose the yurta of a prince.

And gazing from afar, Chotong beheld the fair encampment, and he summoned Sanglun before him, whom he had made his vassal to tend his herds. And he said: "Go thou to the stranger tribe that have pitched their tents on our land, and say to them that for each day's sojourn in the realm of Chotong Khan, they shall yield him tribute of a herd of goodly cattle. But if they will not, he will scatter them like snowflakes on the blast. And the first herd shall be yielded up on the morrow!"

And Sanglun mounted his venerable steed that could scarce support the weight of his master, for he had toiled overlong, and he yearned for ease and the comfort of green pastures, that he might muse on his exploits, singing their

glory to his children's children. But Chotong had ordained that he should serve Sanglun, crying: "Ye are well mated, an ancient beggar and his ancient steed!"

Now as they took their way to the camp of the stranger tribe, the steed broke into speech, saying: "How do my toil-worn bones cry out beneath thee, belovèd master! Had I not been born with a hero's heart in my breast, I were fain to fold my legs upon one another, nor move again from this place."

And Sanglun answered: "Take heart, my friend, and I will beg fodder of yon strangers to comfort thee. If their bounty match their wealth they will not deny me, for never since Gessar left us desolate have I seen so fair a camp."

And from far off Gessar descried the old man on his steed and knew him for Sanglun. And he said to Rogmo: "The old Sanglun draws nigh to parley with us. Do thou welcome him, and bid him eat and drink. Let him be given the hindquarter of an ox and let his tea be proffered him in my bowl of horn, and from behind the hanging I will hearken to all he says."

And Sanglun alighted before the princely yurta and cried: "A courier from Chotong Khan seeks audience here!"

And Rogmo came forth and answered: "What Khan is this and what greeting doth he send us?"

"He that is Khan of Tibet through his evil deeds bids me say to thy lord that for each day's sojourn within his borders ye shall yield him tribute of a herd of goodly cattle. But if ye will not, he will scatter you like snowflakes on the blast. And the first herd shall be yielded up on the morrow!"

"It is well, father, and when my lord is returned from the chase, he shall hear the word of thy master. But now thou art weary, and within the yurta are meat and drink for thy pleasure. Enter and feast!"

"Fain would I enter and feast, kind youth, but first I would beg fodder for my steed, whose hunger is greater than mine!"

"He shall have such fodder as the steeds of heaven crop on Sumeru's cliffs!" And Rogmo clapped her hands together, and straightway a green meadow appeared before them, where lotus flowers bloomed and golden wheat, and in the shadow of wide-spreading trees rivulets flowed. And Sanglun led his steed to the green meadow, but for himself, he entered into the yurta.

And there on a cloth of felt a feast was laid of the hind-quarter of an ox, and savory tea steamed in a bowl of horn. And when Sanglun beheld the ox he laughed aloud, for since he had served Chotong he had eaten naught save roots and bitter herbs, and drunk the dregs of cauldrons.

And from behind the hanging Gessar saw how he tore the flesh with his hands, and sorrow smote him, and he flung to Sanglun the crystal-hafted blade that hung at his girdle. And seeing the blade, Sanglun wept bitterly.

And having eaten, he lifted to his mouth the savory tea and laughed aloud. But marking the bowl of horn where-from he drank, his tears flowed into his beard.

And Rogmo cried: "It hath been said that laughter should be welcomed, but weeping forsworn. Wherefore didst thou laugh at sight of the ox's flesh but weep at sight of the blade? Wherefore didst thou laugh at sight of the savory tea but weep at sight of the bowl?"

And Sanglun answered: "I could not choose but laugh at sight of the flesh and of the savory tea, for since I serve Chotong, I have eaten naught save roots and bitter herbs, and drunk the dregs of cauldrons. But when I beheld the crystal-hafted blade and the bowl of horn, I knew them for Gessar Khan's, and I could not choose but weep, for my heart cried out: 'Thy blade and thy bowl are returned, my son, but thou art perished.'"

Now Gessar, hearing his words, was filled with compassion, and he came forth from behind the hanging and said: "Weep no longer, for Gessar is not dead, but lives. He will return to avenge thy wrongs and the wrongs of his people, and ye shall rejoice with the joy of the shining gods. But now ride back to Chotong, nor let aught of what thou hast heard escape thy lips. And for thy goodwife, take this carcass of a sheep, that she too may eat."

And Rogmo led Sanglun forth from the yurta. And the magic field had vanished, but a steed pawed at the earth, whose eyes flashed fire and whose mane and tail were as silken banners in the wind, and on whose stalwart limbs Sanglun beheld the saddle and bridle that had decked his ancient steed.

And he cried: "This is a steed fit for the gods to ride. But where is the faithful comrade that bore me hither?"

And the steed answered: "Dost thou not know me, master? I am the faithful comrade that bore thee hither, but I

188

have eaten of such fodder as the steeds of heaven crop on Sumeru's cliffs, and I am grown fair as they."

And when Sanglun had bestrode him, he bounded forward, and the old man smote him over the thigh with the sheep's carcass, crying aloud: "Will Gessar return indeed? Or is this a dream that I dreamed as I lay in slumber?"

And the steed answered: "No dream is this, for hast thou not the carcass of a sheep, and who until now hath vouchsafed thee so much as a skin to shelter thee from the cold?"

And the heart of Sanglun was uplifted, and he spurred his steed onward, till they came to where Chotong sat on Gessar's throne, awaiting his coming. And forgetful of the command that had been laid upon him, Sanglun cried out: "Beware, thou son of evil, that hast usurped the throne of the mighty one! For Gessar's name shall blossom as the lotus flower, but the name of Chotong shall be as a torch that is quenched and trampled into the mire!"

And Chotong cried: "For such brave words thou shalt have brave blows, my brother!" And he commanded that Sanglun be beaten with staves of fresh-hewn wood, and having been beaten, he was borne to his yurta of black felt and flung to the earth.

And Amurtsheela wept to see his hurts, crying: "Alas, my husband, thy wounds flow red with thy blood, but where is our son that should avenge thy wrongs?"

And Sanglun answered: "In the tent of the stranger tribe I beheld the crystal-hafted knife that was wont to hang from Gessar's girdle, and the bowl of horn wherefrom he was wont to drink. And one said to me: 'Gessar is not dead, but lives. He will return to avenge thy wrongs and the wrongs of his people, and ye shall rejoice with the joy of the shining gods.' And beneath my robe is the carcass of a sheep that he gave me to stay thy hunger. Therefore be comforted and eat of the carcass, and lay thee down and sleep." And Amurtsheela ate of the carcass, and laid her down and slept.

But on the morrow she betook herself to the camp of the stranger tribe, and from far off Gessar descried her, but he knew her not, for her countenance was veiled with many veils. And he went forth to greet her, crying: "What is thy will of us?"

And she answered: "The all-conquering, all-healing Gessar Khan is my well-loved son, and the gods gave him power to transform himself according to his desire, yet forbade him, whatsoever shape he took, to disguise the five and forty teeth wherewith he was born." And Amurtsheela drew the veils from her countenance, crying: "As I am thy mother, so art thou my son."

And Gessar cried: "I would have lain hidden from thee, good mother, till I had avenged thee!" And he embraced her thrice, and Amurtsheela wept and laughed in turn, and knew not for joy whether she woke or dreamed.

Then Gessar counselled her, saying: "Do thou scale with Rogmo yonder height that overlooks all the valley, and ye shall see how Gessar metes out justice to traitors!"

And Amurtsheela scaled, with the Lady Rogmo, the height that overlooked all the valley, and beheld how Gessar mounted his lowly ass and took his way to Chotong.

Now the vile Chotong sat enthroned at the portal of his yurta, awaiting the stranger's coming. And Gessar approached, but he drove no herd before him, nor did he dismount to pay homage to Chotong, but gazed upon him and spoke no word.

And Chotong cried: "Where is the herd of cattle that I commanded of thee, and wherefore dost thou sit astride thy beast, nor bow to me in homage?"

"I bow to the gods, and I heed the commands of the Everlasting Ones, but none beside."

"And who art thou, rash fool, that dares brave the wrath of the glorious Chotong?"

"I am one that hath adventured through many lands and encountered many perils, and I am come to mete out justice to the vile Chotong."

And Gessar flung off the semblance of a merchant and sat in splendor astride the brown wonder-steed, clad in his armor that was fashioned of seven jewels and sparkled like the dew at dawn. And his helmet, wrought of the woven light of the sun and moon, decked his noble head, and his ebon bow was girded about his shoulders, and thirty silver arrows, turquoise-notched, lay in his quiver. And drawing his lightning-sword three fathoms long, from its sheath, he advanced upon Chotong.

But Chotong fled from before him into the yurta, and creeping within a sack, bound fast its mouth. And Gessar cried: "Let a white cloud come from the east as large as a sheep! Let a black cloud come from the west as large as a heifer!" And in the east a white cloud appeared as large as a sheep, and in the west a black cloud as large as a heifer. And each sped swiftly to meet the other, and crashing together, they released a whirlwind that descended to the earth and tore the yurta from over the head of Chotong, and bore it aloft to the mountain ridge where Rogmo and Amurtsheela held their watch, and set it unharmed beside them.

And Gessar alighted from his steed, and approaching the sack wherein Chotong lay hidden, he cried: "This sack is foul with vermin! Let us drive them forth!" And he thrust his blade through its side.

And the sack trembled, but no sound issued from its depths. And Gessar thrust in his blade a second time, more deeply than before, and the sack rolled from side to side but no sound came forth. And now he thrust his blade in to the hilt, and a stream of blood gushed from within and a voice cried out: "No vermin are here, but thy kinsman Chotong, whom thou hast sorely wounded." And he crept forth out of the sack.

And Gessar cried: "Whose kinsman was Shikeer when thou didst betray him into the hands of the three Shiraigol Khans? Was he not thine? Whose kinsman was Gessar Khan when thou didst deliver up to his enemy his chosen wife? Was he not thine? Woe, woe to thee, for my wrath is as a burning fire that leaps to heaven and will not be quenched save by thy blood, Chotong!" And Gessar advanced upon him with a drawn sword.

But ere he could strike, Sanglun flung himself down before him and cried: "Dread son of heaven! For his evil deeds this traitor hath earned death a hundredfold, by sword and flame and the lashing of many scourges. Yet he is my brother and of noble blood and thy near kinsman. Wherefore, I pray thee, curb thine exceeding wrath, and do with him as thou wilt, but slay him not."

And Gessar answered: "Because I love thee, I will not slay him," and sheathing his sword, he raised Sanglun from the earth and embraced him thrice.

And he cried to his wonder-steed: "Gulp down the traitor Chotong nine times and release him again, that he may be drained of his power whereby he was wont to wreak evil upon his fellows."

And the brown wonder-steed did as Gessar bade him, and when his task was done, Chotong lay on the earth nor rose therefrom, for his strength was less than the strength that abides in a hair.

And now Gessar cried to Sanglun: "Lead me to the battlefield where the thirty heroes perished for my sake."

And Sanglun led him to the battlefield that was strewn with the bones of the thirty heroes, and Gessar, beholding them, broke forth into lamentations, crying: "Where art thou, Nantsong my Falcon, ever eager to rush into the forefront of battle? And thou, Shumar, Eagle among warriors, laughing as thou didst hurl back the ranks of the enemy? Where art thou, my Tiger-hero and flaming Bodotshi and all my comrades that were as the talons of the lion to me, and as torches that light the darkness? With hearts like boulders ye repelled the foe till ye were betrayed and slaughtered, while I, that should have led you into battle, idled in the land of the twelve-headed giant, vanquished by Aralgo's guile!" And for weeping, Gessar could scarce give utterance to his sorrow, and for grief Sanglun could scarce hear his words.

But the brown wonder-steed chided his master, crying: "Ever dost thou lament, my Gessar, till one, knowing thee not, might say a woman's soul dwelt in thy body and no valiant hero's. Spend not thy strength in tears, but entreat thy sisters on Sumeru that they may sue to Kormuzda for the lives of thy heroes."

And Gessar scattered incense upon the earth and poured forth a drink-offering of the blood of a goat. And he cried: "My glorious sisters, when I left your abode and the abode of the shining gods by Buddha's will, thirty matchless comrades bore me company. Where are my comrades now?"

And the voice of his sisters descended to him from above and answered him: "We will betake ourselves to thy father Kormuzda, and sue to him for the lives of thy matchless comrades."

And the three sisters betook themselves to Kormuzda, where he sat enthroned among the three and thirty gods that served him. And they bowed nine times, striking their hands together, and cried: "Father of the gods and servant of Buddha's will! Our brother is returned from the land of the Shiraigol Khans, and weeps on the battlefield where his thirty heroes lie slain, and will not be comforted."

And Kormuzda answered: "Had he not forsaken his heroes to follow after the Lady Aralgo, he would not now be mourning their death. Yet it is written in the book of destiny that the servants shall mourn their master, not the

master his servants. Wherefore I will go to him that orders all things, and learn his will."

And Kormuzda went to him that orders all things, and kneeling before him, spoke: "Thou jewel in the lotus flower! My son, who by thy will descended in mortal guise to rule the earth, hath served thee well, having destroyed the seven alwins and slain the Wild Boar of the Wilderness and put to death the giant with twelve heads and all his kin. Yet now he weeps on the battlefield where his thirty heroes lie bereft of life at the hand of the Shiraigol Khans, and he will not be comforted. And since it hath been written in the book of destiny, O holy vessel of truth, that the servants shall mourn their master, not the master his servants, I am come hither in humbleness to learn thy will."

And he that dispenses justice to gods and men smiled upon Kormuzda and answered: "Because for two hundred years thou wert forgetful of the command I laid upon thee, therefore doth thy son now weep over the bones of his lost comrades. Yet I will have compassion upon him, and transform his weeping to laughter and his sorrow to joy through the power of the blessèd arshaan."

And from a bowl of ivory that held the blessèd arshaan, Buddha filled a golden chalice, and gave the chalice into Kormuzda's hand, saying: "Let thy son besprinkle the bones of his heroes with this holy fluid, and the bones shall be joined together, and the sinews shall knit themselves upon one another, and the flesh shall cover them. Let him besprinkle them a second time, and the breath of life shall enter into their bodies, making them whole. Let him besprinkle them a third time, and they shall be born anew and rise from the earth."

And Kormuzda took the chalice from the hand of the Mighty One and returned to his dwelling-place where the three glorious sisters awaited him. And he gave the golden chalice into their keeping, together with the word that the Lord Buddha had spoken to him, and they descended earthward.

And when they came to the battlefield where Gessar wept over the bones of his heroes, they cried: "Because it is written in the book of destiny that the servants shall mourn their master, not the master his servants, the Lord Buddha hath sent thee in a golden chalice the blessèd arshaan. Besprinkle the bones of thy heroes with this holy fluid, and the bones shall be joined together, and the sinews shall knit themselves upon one another, and the flesh shall cover them. Besprinkle them a second time, and the breath of life shall enter into their bodies, making them whole. Besprinkle them a third time, and they shall be born anew and rise from the earth. This is the word of Buddha to Kormuzda's son!"

And hearing this word, the soul of Gessar was flooded with radiance, and he bowed in worship nine times nine times before the All-Compassionate One, and nine times before his father Kormuzda, and taking the blessèd arshaan from the hand of his sisters, he cried: "Ye glorious ones, whose love hath followed me as the shadow my body, may ye be honored above all the dakeeni and your souls be bathed in the sacred blue of the skies!"

And he besprinkled the bones of his heroes with the

blessed arshaan, and the bones were joined together, and the sinews knit themselves upon one another, and the flesh covered them. And he besprinkled them a second time, and the breath of life entered into their bodies, making them whole. And he besprinkled them a third time, and they were born anew and rose from the earth and bowed in thanksgiving to the gods.

Then they surrounded Gessar and, kneeling before him, kissed the hem of his robe and cried: "Thou son of heaven, uprooter of the tenfold evil, lord over all the creatures of the earth, light-spreading Gessar Khan! When the enemy descended upon us, we overthrew him and slew many brave warriors and took captive many herds of steed, for though thou wert not by to lead us into battle, did not the noble Shikeer command us? Yet when at dawn they stole upon us as we slumbered, so heavy were our eyes with sleep and our limbs with drinking that our strength prevailed not against them and we perished on the battlefield. But now the blessèd Buddha hath restored us, wherefore weep no longer, dear master, but raise us from the earth and rejoice!"

And Gessar raised them from the earth, embracing each in turn, and cried: "My thirty heroes are restored to me in all their strength and beauty. Yet where is he that commanded you, where is the grey-flecked hawk that came to me in the wilderness, where is Shikeer my brother?"

And Shikeer, with the head of a man and the body and tail of a hawk, flew down from the heavens and alighted on Gessar's hand.

And Gessar cried: "Behold, Shikeer, the blessèd arshaan

that the Lord Buddha hath sent to restore the thirty heroes to life! Thee it will restore to mortal form, if so be thou dost crave this boon."

But Shikeer made answer: "How should I crave it, Gessar, for my arm is wearied by the blows that I dealt at the Chatun Stream, and the wound at my throat throbs with a bitter pain, and my heart weeps for the evil deeds of men. Nay, brother, if it please thee, I would return to the abode of the high gods, nor dwell again upon earth."

And Gessar answered: "Let it be so, Shikeer! Do thou return to the abode of the high gods, and my sisters will go before thee and Kormuzda my father will take thee by the hand and give thee surcease from pain."

And Shikeer bade farewell to Gessar and the thirty heroes and his father Sanglun, and soared aloft. And the three sisters went before him, and when they reached the abode of the high gods, Kormuzda took Shikeer by the hand and gave him surcease from pain. And his wingèd charger galloped forth from the heavenly stalls to greet him, and Shikeer dwelt with him henceforth on Sumeru, nor descended again to earth.

But Gessar Khan commanded that a feast be prepared, and the thirty heroes were bidden thereto and the three hundred chieftains of the tribes, together with all their tribesmen, and the Lady Rogmo sat at the right hand of Gessar, and Sanglun sat beside her, and at his left hand Amurtsheela sat.

And for three moons they feasted, and the sound of their revelry was borne over all the land and to the deepest caverns of the sea. And clouds of fragrant incense floated upward in tribute to the gods, and by night the radiant lingho-blossom opened its chalice, lighting the darkness.

And when the feast was done, and the merry-making, and the heroes and chieftains were returned to their abodes, the all-conquering, all-healing son of heaven, the glorious Gessar Khan, ascended his golden throne, bearing the sword of righteousness in one hand and in the other hand the balm of peace. And having uprooted the tenfold evil and restored gladness to the hearts of men, he dwelt among them in the wisdom and joy of the gods, ruling over his people as the sun rules in the heavens and as the mountain rules over the valley below.

Thus ends the tale of the hero Gessar Khan.

EXPLANATION OF FOREIGN WORDS USED IN TEXT

Alwin—A kind of evil being.

Arshaan—Holy saffron water.

Assuri—Evil spirits that lived in the cleft of the world mountain Sumeru.

Baling—A figure shaped like a pyramid and kneaded of dough, often brought as an offering to the dead.

Chigitai—A kind of wild horse.

Dakeeni—Goddesses.

Shimnu—A demonic spirit.

Yaksha—A witch.

MORE FOLK TALES
FROM PILGIRMS PUBLISHING

www.pilgrimsbooks.com

For catalog and more information mail or fax to:

PILGRIMS BOOK HOUSE

Mail Order, P. O. Box 3872, Kathmandu, Nepal
Tel: 977-1-4700919 Fax: 977-1-4700943
E-mail: mailorder@pilgrims.wlink.com.np